Everyone is trying to sell someth ̄ ̄ ̄ ̄ ̄ ̄ ̄ ̄. *Life Is Sales: Change Your Life—Be More Persuasive and Get What You Want* says that we are all walking advertisements—about what we, as humans, can do for one another. Confidence is the winning marketing strategy when dealing with others, and Ford and Bird seek to explain the psychology behind it and how you can use the marketing skills picked up in this book to change one's life. *Life Is Sales* is a complex and highly recommended look at selling oneself for a better life.

—*Midwest Book Review*

I have read numerous sales books. I must sincerely say that I would definitely put *Life Is Sales* on my list as highly recommended. The language used in the book [is] very easy to comprehend. They also provide valuable tips, insights, [and] examples to use in your daily sales life. This book will also be enjoyed by those who are not in the sales profession. Thanks, Gary and Connie, for this great book.

—Nissar Ahamed

Life Is Management

Also by the author

Life Is Sales
with Connie Bird

The Canadian Guide to Protecting Yourself from
Identity Theft and Other Fraud
with Graham McWaters

Life Is Management

Coaching Extraordinary Performance from Everyone

Gary L. Ford

INSOMNIAC PRESS

Library and Archives Canada Cataloguing in Publication

Ford, Gary, 1946-

Ford, Gary, 1946-
    Life is management / Gary Ford.

ISBN 978-1-55483-103-6

    1. Employees--Coaching of. 2. Management.
3. Organizational change. I. Title.

HF5549.5.C53F67 2013   658.3'124   C2013-901470-5

The publisher gratefully acknowledges the support of the Department of Canadian Heritage through the Book Publishing Industry Development Program.

Printed and bound in Canada

Insomniac Press
520 Princess Avenue
London, Ontario, Canada, N6B 2B8
www.insomniacpress.com

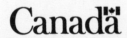

Contents

Life Is Management

When I first became a manager, I thought I knew it all. I was over-confident in my skills and knowledge. I was full of bright new ideas and eager to help shape the company in new and exciting directions. I had a tendency to second-guess the decisions made by the leadership of the company and felt compelled to share my thoughts at management meetings. I just couldn't understand why they didn't act on every one of my suggestions for improvement.

Finally, my VP at the time took me aside and said, "You are a new manager, and I applaud your enthusiasm and eagerness to help change the company, but you are not running the company just yet and therefore I need you to focus your energies on what you can accomplish in your own department. If you keep looking for all the wrong things with our company, you will find them, but if you look for the things that are right with this company, you will find those too and become a major contributor in building our company into a world-class player. We can't do it all immediately, but we can work on things within our own environment. I encourage you to focus your energies on building on what we are good at so we become exceptional."

These few words changed my life, and I refocused my exuberance onto those things I could control. These words helped me become a better manager and later a better executive. They allowed me to write this book. Mind you, I still popped out the odd off-the-wall idea at meetings, and some of them actually took root and did have an impact on our company. I just didn't do it every day. I became more thoughtful and, I think, a better manager.

In my first book, *Life Is Sales*, I indicate that all of us want to influence or persuade others in order to get more of what we want in life. In *Life Is Management*, I take some of the same principles and apply them to the management of people. There are really only three key priorities in business: hiring potential results-getters, keeping results-getters, and developing results-getters. Managers deliver on all three counts.

All managers want to influence those who work with them in order to increase profits, increase sales, increase performance, improve service, or have employees reach their potential for the overall betterment of the company. Management guru Peter Drucker is well known for defining management as "getting things done through other people." The power of influence and persuasion, therefore, is conducted through other people. Giving orders only works short term and usually only delivers mediocre results at best. Influencing employees to want to meet corporate priorities is much more effective in getting things done and has a long-term impact on performance.

I believe there is a significant difference between leadership and management. This book will deal with management as it pertains to getting things done. Leaders inspire while managers meet the day-to-day goals and objectives of the company. Leaders set strategy while managers execute this strategy. Leaders establish priorities while managers deliver the results. Many confuse leadership with management, and this usually leads to unfocused activities, which limit a company's success. They are two totally different functions within a company and should operate separately to maximize performance. Expert managers are perhaps more vital to a company's success than expert leaders. Leadership without execution is a recipe for failure. Execution without vision is also a recipe for disaster. It has often been said, however, that a poor strategy well executed is better than an excellent strategy poorly executed. The two work hand in glove to deliver superior performance.

There are many books on leadership but few really good books on management. This is one of those good books on management. If great leaders are born, then great managers are made. *Life Is Management* provides clear, precise, and practical instructions on how to make you a great manager.

You will gain insights into the role of a manager with the help of concrete examples and lists of the best practices that will elevate every manager's performance. We will deal with the common sense issues regarding the role of managers. Once the basic role is defined, it becomes much easier to execute superior performance. Getting extraordinary results from everyone is the number one goal of every manager, and having a well-defined coaching process as outlined in this book will get you there. The highly successful businessperson and founder of Mary Kay Cosmetics, Mary Kay Ash, is quoted as having said, "There are two things people want more than sex and money: recognition and praise." We will delve into the psychology of human nature and how we can apply it to the role of manager and coach.

You will be more successful when you implement these simple yet effective strategies into your management life. These strategies don't simply apply to your work life; they also apply to all aspects of day-to-day living. We are all managers of some aspect of our life besides work. We may be a part of a charitable organization where we have to manage fundraising; we manage our family finances; we attempt to manage our teenagers; we may be involved in our church or golf club. All require us to get things done through other people. We must be influential in these roles because we need to get things done without power. Getting things done without authority is a true sign of an excellent manager.

It's interesting to observe managers who have been recently promoted. These new managers are excited about the promotion and keen to do good work to justify the company's faith in the decision. Most companies select good employees to promote. These are employees who have excelled at their job but may not have demonstrated any managerial expertise. These new managers get minimal training and are expected to manage a group of employees and deliver results. These managers are so keen that they feel it's their job to help their employees be better at their jobs, so they observe employee performance carefully.

And what are they looking for? Most managers look for employees doing something wrong so they can fix it. Their desire to improve matters is admirable, but they focus most of their attention on things that employees are no good at. After a few years in the role, these managers wonder why their hard efforts at improving performance show little success. These attempts at improving performance by focusing on things employees are no good at produce minimal results. You may wonder why. It seems to make good sense to help people get better at things they're not good at. The main reason why employees don't improve much in this case is because *they are no good at it*. Attempting to eliminate weaknesses is a natural response for all managers who want to improve performance. Building on strengths, however, is a much more successful approach in improving performance.

Competence builds confidence
Confidence builds behaviours
Behaviours build results

We will spend considerable time on this philosophy as we discuss the various methods available to help managers get things done through other people. Coaching behavioural change yields results. I will introduce you to the most effective coaching process that has been field-tested by some of the most effective companies in the world.

Inexperienced managers also believe that employees should do what they're told. The style of new managers usually includes a more autocratic approach. Authority comes with the title, or so they think. Granted, a dictatorship may be the most efficient form of government, but it's certainly not the most effective. Many managers never graduate from this autocratic style. They in turn never reach their true potential, and their employees slowly drift away to other managers or other companies. Employees rarely leave the company; they usually leave the manager.

There are so many different approaches to management because it's such a personal function. Dealing with people is a necessary challenge in the business world. Numbers have a defined logic to them, but people react in such a variety of ways that the manager's role is a challenging one. Great managers are few and far between while mediocre managers are commonplace. All of us have experienced bad managers, and there are far too many of these bad managers running our companies today. They are bad for a variety of reasons, but the great managers are great because of a few very specific skills they have developed throughout their careers. This book focuses on these skills. It will give you the tools you need to build a successful career.

While the skills outlined in this book will make you a better manager at work, it will also make you a better parent and a better spouse everywhere; in fact, you will be better in every aspect of your life. After all, *life is management.*

Chapter 1
We Are All Managers

Life is management. We all have some natural capacity to manage things or manage people. Have a look at your life, and you will see that you already demonstrate management skills in some aspect. You manage the family budget, your work–life balance, your diet, your children, your relationships with friends and colleagues. You are able to execute a plan, and you get things done through other people.

My daughter is a schoolteacher. She teaches grade five. If you remember what you were like in grade five, you will readily agree that management skills are paramount in teaching an unruly group of little children in that delicate stage between child and adolescent. It's a challenge to maintain control over the talkative ones without reducing their enthusiasm and to encourage the quiet ones to participate without making them feel embarrassed, all the while creating an atmosphere conducive to learning.

James (not his real name) was an eager student in her class. He always wanted to answer every question, and would even answer on the behalf of others. He was your classic class clown and disruptive to the other students. Many teachers manage this kind of student with harsher and harsher rules, and these students tend to spend a lot of time at the principal's office. I can personally attest that going to the principal's office has a huge impact on behaviour, but only for a day.

My daughter, on the other hand, looked at James's strengths rather than all his disruptive behaviour. It's difficult to reason with someone in grade five, as their sense of logic hasn't developed fully. Many managers will say they have employees just like James, and after two years of progressive discipline, they usually end up firing them. These managers haven't learned the best practices of management.

Good managers and good teachers alike build on good qualities rather than try to eliminate the bad. Building on strengths will be a common theme throughout the book as we focus on building your managerial skills. This same strategy applies to your own skills as well. Find those things you're good at, those things you enjoy, and build on them to become an exceptional manager.

My own son Michael was a difficult student. He was disruptive, liked to talk and socialize in class, and rarely handed in quality work. His marks were disappointing to say the least. We worked with him at home and provided discipline around study time, but he always found a way to avoid the work and much preferred to play. I'm sure most parents can relate to this challenge. Our objective was to make sure Michael became a better student and capitalized on the learning opportunities in school. Our secondary objective was to ensure that Michael learned how to learn and then apply that knowledge to get better grades.

Like most parents, our first approach was to look at all the things he was doing wrong and try to eliminate those. Not enough study time? Our answer was to schedule study time for him. Poor marks? We would review all the wrong answers and try to find out what he did wrong. We tried logic: paying attention in class was important to his future. Too much playtime was resolved by limiting TV and video games. All of our efforts had minimal effect because we were focusing on what was wrong rather than what was right. As parents, we were using the autocratic approach to manage Michael's behaviour.

Finally, in grade six, Michael found a teacher who knew how

to manage students. This teacher realized that Michael was disruptive because he was bored. Michael needed a challenge, and that is exactly what happened. The teacher decided to build on Michael's strengths rather than focus on his weaknesses. Michael was creative, energetic, and intelligent. When he faced challenges that appealed to these traits, something exciting happened.

Michael responded to the management skills of his teacher, and his marks skyrocketed. He started to like school, and he focused his overabundant energies on schoolwork. This teacher changed Michael's behaviour, and to this day, Michael appreciates these very management skills that turned him onto education. This teacher did this with many other students too, as he took a personal approach to teaching rather than an autocratic one. A great teacher is also a great manager.

My daughter Jennifer applied the same approach to her student James. This boy was full of energy and had a keen desire for attention. How could she build on this strength to help James become a productive member of the class and contribute to the learning environment? She decided to give him some simple jobs in the classroom that encouraged him to keep busy and also gave him a sense of contribution. He no longer needed to act out to gain attention, as he was being acknowledged for all his help. He settled down quickly to focus on the learning. Jennifer made a big difference in James's performance by simply shifting her focus from what he was doing wrong to what he could do right.

Your employees will respond the same way once you take the time to learn what their strengths are and then let them build their skills from a strengths-based premise rather than a weakness-based premise.

Behavioural Change

Getting behavioural change is the objective of every good manager. We see examples of this ability everywhere in our own personal lives. A number of years ago, I had a manager, Bill (not his real name), who was a "by the book" manager. He expected his employees to do exactly what they were told. His employees didn't like him much but respected his expertise and knowledge. They followed his commands without question, as they feared his reprimands. They showed no initiative in resolving client issues without his approval. Service declined in his unit as a result. Bill's response was to become even more autocratic and, yes, even nasty. The annual performance review was a time for fear rather than anticipation. Some employees actually got physically ill the day before the review. It was a difficult situation for me, as Bill was an experienced manager who knew our products and service better than anyone in the company.

I had managed Bill for four years and was getting to the end of my rope with him. My approach had been to use a two-by-four management technique that basically exercised my authority over him. He would be much improved for about two months but would slip back into his usual pattern. Four months later, I would pull out the two-by-four again. I didn't like it, but it seemed to work at the time for short-term results. I didn't really understand the impact his style was having on his employees until years later when employees who had left the company confided in me why they had left.

Bill was a member of a private golf club and had worked hard on the board of directors until he became president of the club. Previously, his success at the club was achieved by doing it all himself. When he became president, he needed others to help him get things done. He tried the autocratic approach but discovered quickly that other members didn't respect his authority and simply refused to fall in line. This was a rude awakening for Bill. This approach had worked on the job, but at the club, he had no consequences to deliver, so he had no power.

How to manage without power was a real challenge for Bill, so we chatted about how to get things done through other people and without authority. He experimented with some of the principles of influence that are covered in this book and discovered he could catch more flies with honey rather than vinegar. He started to listen and compromise, and he learned to empower members of the board. They responded and started to get things done. The success he had with this new approach led him to try expanding on it. He had an outstanding year as president and received accolades from the membership.

Did Bill transfer this newfound management skill to his job? I'm afraid not. He just couldn't get past the notion that the manager must know it all and must keep employees in line. He actually got even more autocratic, and staff started to leave and customers complained. Unfortunately, we had to let Bill go. He had failed to capitalize on what he learned as president of the golf course, but the failure was also mine.

Bill's termination proved to be the best thing for him, as it finally sunk in that his style was destructive to the success of the company. He has since changed careers and found his niche. He has actually turned into a far better manager now. The harsh reality of termination sometimes opens the door to new and improved behaviour.

Learn to Be a Better Manager

The message here is simple. We all have management strengths and have management experience in our lives. Find what works in your life and build on this skill to enhance your career. The best way to learn is to take on a volunteer role and learn to manage without authority. It seems the title of manager imbues too many of us with the notion that we should be in charge and therefore be autocratic. When we manage without authority, we must learn how to get things done through other people. Rather than issue the threat of reprimand, we must do this through influence and persuasion. You will soon learn that these skills are invaluable to every manager who wants success.

Chapter 2
Leadership vs. Management

Do you want to be a leader or a manager? Most leadership books talk about leadership as a CEO while most of the readers don't aspire to be a CEO but do want to be more effective in their jobs. There is a definite difference between leadership and management, and there is a definite myth about this difference.

An oft-quoted phrase tells us that "leadership is doing the right things and management is doing things right." This illustrates how the two skill sets need to work together. If you want to be well rounded, you must have the ability to manage the day-to-day tasks and deliver results while seeing the big picture and opportunities for change. Demonstrating good leadership skills without the management skills to support them will leave you with an inability to deliver on your vision as a leader. Likewise, being a good manager without good leadership skills will constantly lead to challenges in motivating your team and producing the results you are trying to manage. Successfully blending these two styles requires a truly powerful skill set. Keep in mind that there are many managers in the world, but very few truly embody the characteristics of a leader.

Most of us have worked for managers who have no leadership skills. They are merely conduits for what the so-called leaders of the organization want. They lack the thought processes that deliver the strategy at the ground level of an organization. The following list was developed in the book *Learning to Lead: A Workbook on Becoming a Leader* by Warren Bennis, a popular writer of leadership resources and business professor at the University of Southern California. He highlights some of the common myths about management. Many authors downplay the role of managers and highlight the role of leaders. Have a look at this list and see if you agree.

- The manager administers; the leader innovates.
- The manager maintains; the leader develops.
- The manager accepts reality; the leader investigates it.
- The manager focuses on systems and structures; the leader focuses on people.
- The manager relies on control; the leader inspires trust.
- The manager has a short-range view; the leader has a long-range perspective.
- The manager asks how and when; the leader asks what and why.
- The manager has their eye always on the bottom line; the leader has their eye on the horizon.
- The manager imitates; the leader originates.
- The manager accepts the status quo; the leader challenges it.
- The manager is the classic good soldier; the leader is their own person.

Bennis summarizes the difference between management and leadership as follows:

> There is a profound difference between management and leadership, and both are important. To manage means to bring about, to accomplish, and to have charge of or responsibility for, to conduct. Leading is influencing, guiding in a direction, course, action, and opinion. The distinction is crucial.

One of Bennis's most quoted phrases is, "Managers are people who do things right and leaders are people who do the right thing." It would seem that leaders are much higher on the evolutionary scale than mere managers. Recent history in assessing the leadership qualities of companies such as General Motors, Lehman Brothers, Enron, etc., would indicate that leaders do not always do the right things. They often do the wrong thing because they are focused on short-term profits rather than long-term growth.

A Good Idea Is Only As Good As Its Implementation

It would appear that a mediocre strategy well executed is far superior to an excellent strategy poorly implemented. So who is responsible for the implementation? That's right. The managers. They make things happen.

I'm always amazed when looking at bank branches in particular. The bank company will have the same leadership, the same strategy, and yet the performance and service levels are vastly different branch to branch. I believe the bulk of leadership books on the market target the wrong audience. It's managers who influence the daily performance of any company; they deliver directly to the buying consumer. No matter how elegant the company strategy, if the management team fails to deliver, the company fails too.

Let's take a closer look at management skills as a subset of leadership—or perhaps more important, leadership as a subset of management. Many executives will try to distinguish themselves by saying that they are leaders, not managers. Alarm bells should go off when we hear these words. In my experience, the people who say this generally fail when it comes to attracting followers, which makes it difficult to consider them successful leaders.

A leader is someone who knows where to go. Management skills are how they actually get there. A friend of mine organized a three-day fishing trip up north. He acted as a leader as he created the vision of the trip and where to go, but he acted as a manager in providing clear directions to the fishing camp, outlining how expensive it would be, picking people who could reasonably be expected to get along, and coordinating the trip with the facility. These were all management roles. If he had failed, it would have been one sad trip, as some of us might have ended up in the wrong location with the wrong fishing gear. (It was a wonderful trip, by the way.)

Someone who tries to act as a leader but wants nothing to do with management is like my seven-year-old granddaughter finding the keys to the family car and being overwhelmed with the desire to drive to McDonald's for some Chicken McNuggets and fries. There is a clear vision and goal with a strong sense of purpose and desire to attain that goal, but the ability to plan and execute the trip is lacking.

I once worked for someone who wanted to lead but not manage. They tried to explain this by saying that they were "a visionary." I suppose that they meant they came up with the ideas and other people executed them, but the *Merriam-Webster* definition of a visionary suggests that they are "one whose ideas or projects are impractical." That's a pretty good description of someone who wants to lead but not manage. Basically, the visionary has no accountability for results. Have you noticed that many visionaries quite often change their visions, leaving the rest of us wondering where we are going? The visionary may have wonderful ideas, but without the ability to plan and oversee the necessary work, their ideas aren't going to be realized—at least not by them. If their ideas are implemented, it will be a manager who gets it done.

While management is an important part of leadership, the inverse is equally true. Every single team under a manager has its own unique culture and vision of how it can contribute to the company's overall success. Managers who abdicate this leadership role usually end up with employees who just do the bare minimum to survive, and the managers will wonder why their employees are unmotivated. Managers cannot manage and leaders cannot lead without understanding people. Every leader and every manager will become more effective by implementing the people skills based on the psychology of influence and persuasion as outlined in this book.

Leadership defines the culture of the organization, while management instills the culture in the organization. Henry Mintzberg outlines this role of management in his book, *Managing*:

> Managers work involves developing peer relationships, carrying out negotiations, motivating subordinates, resolving conflicts, establishing information networks and disseminating information, making decisions with little or ambiguous information, and allocating resources. These skills are different from but complementary to the more concrete ones required of leaders.

According to the training website Performance Coaching International, the top five concerns workers voice about their managers are:

1. Failure to coach
2. Failure to set clear goals
3. Failure to delegate
4. Failure to celebrate success
5. Inability to show flexibility in leadership style

To get a better idea of how managers affect employees and their performance, let's look at each of these concerns.

Failure to coach. It appears that employees want coaching on a regular and timely basis. The feedback from employees is that they don't receive coaching at all and therefore feel its hindering their effectiveness.

Failure to set clear goals. Clarity of goals is the critical component in communication. When employees don't have clear and concise goals, they can't deliver on the company strategy.

Failure to delegate. Many managers maintain tight control over all aspects of the division and limit the employees' ability to be creative and entrepreneurial. If you delegate responsibility and accountability, your team will respond.

Failure to celebrate success. Work should be fun, and celebrating success encourages your employees to repeat behaviour that's effective. Celebrate often, and reward the behaviour you want.

Inability to show flexibility in leadership style. Employees expect managers to be flexible and to listen to their concerns and opportunities. Inflexible managers produce inflexible employees who can't deliver the kind of service clients expect. Lead by example and show your flexability.

A simple test in any organization is to ask employees what the vision statement of the company is. Executives think employees know, but time and again it's discovered that they don't have a clue.

Time Management

Managers and leaders are being bogged down with unnecessary time-consuming work and are failing to coach their people to top performance. The mantra of "more with less" is having an impact on the personal growth of people and in turn on the performance of the company. In discussions I had with managers while working on this book, it became clear that their administrative workload has increased significantly. They have more documents, not fewer; they have more meetings, not fewer; they have to justify more decisions not fewer. When asked what their number one challenge is as a manager, it was time management. Most managers want to do a good job and want to communicate effectively with their teams, but time pressures are such that they can't seem to fit it into their schedules. So coaching suffers, personal development suffers, and their own work–life balance suffers.

Email may well be part of the issue, as information overload is prevalent in most companies. It seems we want ever more information before we make a decision. Email replaces personal interaction, and more people are using "reply all" to ensure everyone is up to date. All this does is create a bureaucratic environment that hinders the management of people and focuses on managing things. What do you do when your email pings at your desk or your smartphone vibrates? Most of us stop what we're doing and check it. This is probably the biggest time waster there is.

Many managers actually profess a preference for communicating with their staff through email rather than face to face. Technology is wonderful, but don't let it control your relationship with your team. Your people need to be coached—they want to be coached—and they want face-to-face meetings with you. Things get done when you communicate in person.

Meetings are the next biggest time waster. In discussions with managers and employees, virtually all of them admitted that most meetings are a waste of their time, but they feel obliged to attend them. I recommend not attending a meeting if you aren't speaking at it. Meetings are just a conveyor of information, and you can read about it. This could save you enough time to actually coach your people.

Starting meetings on time is another big issue as well. Attendees tend to waste ten minutes waiting for stragglers. Try locking the door one minute after the start time, and see what happens.

Lacking a concrete action plan following a meeting is another waste. Many meetings are established just to set another meeting date. Also consider not inviting so many people. Only include those who have a direct stake in what is being discussed.

For more help in this matter, please see the chapter on time and change management.

If employees don't know the company vision or don't know the goals, how can we expect managers to lead employees toward stated goals when the communication regarding them is so fuzzy? It all comes back to understanding people and coaching these people for improved performance. This book focuses extensively on the power of coaching and how to be more effective with the disciplined process of coaching.

Great managers coach their employees. Great leaders are also great managers and coach their employees. So let's start with how we can become great coaches.

Best Practices

1. Learn to be an effective coach, as employees want coaching.

2. Clarify the corporate goals often.

3. Turn your email off for a total of four hours each day.

4. Walk around your office often to say hello to your staff.

5. Meet with your people in person rather than depend on email.

6. Eliminate "reply all" practices in your office.

7. Celebrate success with your people often and in person.

8. Just be nice.

Chapter 3

What Type of Manager Are You? What Type of Manager Can You Be?

No one can achieve great things without great people. Great managers know how to bring the best out of employees. Each of us has natural styles that have evolved over our lifetime. These styles affect our managerial ability for better or worse. When we focus on strengths and build on them, we can build a team that will achieve greatness. If we merely rely on our natural tendencies, we will have mixed results at best. We can choose to be better managers, and better managers we will become. The choice is yours.

Managers can be divided into two categories. In the sixties, management literature investigated a philosophy called Theory X and Theory Y. Basically, Theory X managers assume people can't be counted on to behave in a responsible, self-managing, and committed manner. Theory Y managers, on the other hand, believe they can count on people to be responsible, committed to the corporate goals, and self-motivated. Your perception of people will influence your management style significantly. Are you a Theory X or a Theory Y manager? What you believe about your people will determine how you manage them. Your style will reinforce what you think about your people in the first place. You will be proven right with both approaches, but one approach is far more successful in getting things done through other people.

Which of the following styles fit your current pattern? Which of them can be added to your personal approach to enhance your performance?

The micromanager. We have all worked with a micromanager, and the experience is never pleasant. I once had a boss who had a definite need to be informed of practically everything. He was so detail-oriented that he wanted a paper trail for every discussion. After a meeting, I would have to document the discussion and send him an email. I often got the email back with a request for more detail. I seemed to spend half my time responding to his detail-oriented requests.

I wasn't allowed to make decisions without checking with him first. The odd time I did make a decision, I was forced to document the entire transaction and the reasons why I made the decision without checking with him. The real challenge in dealing with micromanagers is with their need to be in control. Even when they assign you to a task, they won't tell you everything you need to know to complete it. You could spend hours working on it only to find out that half the information you needed was sitting on your boss's desk the whole time. This is how they maintain control and add to their own importance.

If you say things like the following, I am sorry to tell you, but you're a micromanager:

- "If you can't do it right, I will do it myself."
- "Is this the best you can do?"
- "Put that request in the form of a case study for our consideration."

Micromanagers love details and make decisions slowly and painfully. They love to work overtime to see who else is working.

Being the last to leave is a status symbol. No one likes working for a micromanager. Employees of micromanagers avoid creativity, initiative, and responsibility. They rely on policy and even quote policy to clients. The end results are fewer clients.

Mircomanagers tend to be control freaks who think they are excellent managers that maintain control over their division. They always know what's going on and are proud to tell senior executives how informed they are. My micromanager was excellent at managing up but terrible at managing down. So many micromanagers are in positions of power because they focus on moving up. To maintain their mystique of always being in control, they will rarely admit to not knowing something and have a knack for delaying discussions and decisions until they do know the answers. They have a great deal of difficulty saying, "I don't know; let me check and get back to you."

The good quality of micromanagers, if it can be harnessed, is their ability to monitor progress and make adjustments quickly to meet expectations. They do, however, need to include their team members more often and start believing they can help execute important tasks.

You can learn balance as a micromanager when you micromanage your own personal development. When micromanagers decide to focus on their own professional development, they can be quite focused and successful in bringing balance to their approach, thereby reducing their need for absolute control.

The autocrat. This is perhaps the most common manager. The higher the position, the more likely it will be filled by an autocrat. Autocrats have one objective: their own. They don't care about employees other than using them as stepping stones to advance their careers. Nothing anyone ever does is good enough to satisfy them, and they're almost impossible to get along with. Autocrats want things done their way and only their way. They will go to unusual lengths to make a point.

I remember one manager of mine who had a fetish for posters in windows. They had to be perfectly straight. One day he came into my office, and the posters were slightly unaligned. He immediately jumped on a desk, ripped the posters down, and handed me the crumpled remains. "Put them up straight next time," he said. Needless to say, the posters were perfect from that day on. The story of the incident spread to all facilities, and we never had a crooked poster again. Autocrats can make things happen quickly, and will make examples of people to clarify rules and regulations. They don't suffer fools gladly, and will use sarcastic humour to embarrass employees. They are always right and demand compliance in all aspects of work life. Employees can make decisions, but they had better be the right ones, meaning they had better be aligned with the autocrat's strategy.

Autocrats rarely ask for input on anything and rarely admit to mistakes. Perfection rules! They also seem to have difficulty sharing the limelight. They have difficulty giving praise and may even take your glory for themselves. They are tough to work for, but much can be learned from them. In fact, I probably learned the most from my autocratic boss. He was extremely intelligent and was often right. He was one of the finest inspirational speakers I have ever worked for, but he also could be the most destructive. We just never knew who would show up.

The good qualities of autocrats include being decisive, operating effectively in a crisis situation, and inspiring others with their knowledge and confidence. They are usually marvellous public speakers, as they have such confidence in their own abilities and infallibility. They are fun to watch from afar. However, if you can get past the façade, they are extremely interesting people.

The non-manager. These managers make careers out of having everyone else fix their problems. They take little or no responsibility for their own employees, divisions, or results but are the first to take credit when something does go well. Employees know the non-manager doesn't have their back. When something goes wrong, employees are left alone to face the music. This is why this type of manager has no loyal following.

They play the role of manager but don't really know how to perform. They are deathly afraid of their weak managerial performance being discovered. This fear of being discovered rules their day-to-day life, and it's sad to watch. If your team feels like this about you, it's time to reassess your strengths and build on them to reduce the stress of always finding someone else to blame. Politicians are masters at blaming others and dodging the accountability of their actions, so they rarely get much accomplished.

Non-managers have good intentions and want to be successful, but they haven't developed the skills to do so. Meaning to do well and having the desire to succeed are good qualities that can lead to a more balanced management style with effective coaching. This type of manager has the potential to learn how to become an effective manager without needing to unlearn many bad habits and beliefs already ingrained in other managerial types.

The good guy. Companies are full of sweet managers whose first impression is of an inclusive manager who is wonderful to work for. You will initially get a warm and fuzzy feeling about them, and you'll believe that it's going to be a great job. This manager has a need for affiliation, to be liked. This leads to wishy-washy decisions and to bending company rules to please employees. It also leads to unfair treatment amongst employees, and people resent favouritism.

Good guys struggle with decision-making, as they seek consensus on all decisions. It's easier for them to delay than face the consequences of an unpopular decision. They fold like a cheap suit under confrontation, and autocrats will walk all over them publicly. Good guys will tell you exactly what you want to hear, then turn around and do the exact opposite. In a crisis situation, they will leave you hanging out to dry and will be anything but supportive.

As far as coaching is concerned, good guys are incapable of honest and direct feedback. They are rarely upfront with employees, preferring to just be nice. Results suffer because employees are unclear of the direction of their division and their progress.

Good guys do have redeeming qualities. They are concerned about being appreciated by their employees. They often care about their people deeply but mistake empathy for clear direction and management. This concern over the team's welfare can be a powerful motivator for the team when the manager gains a more balanced approach of being fair and firm with the direction.

The combo manager. In reality, all managers are some combination of the above types. We have many qualities intermixed in our own personal styles. The challenge is knowing when to let one style take more control. In a crisis, we want to lean toward the autocrat because decisive action is required. Shifting cultural norms requires some of the good guy and some of the micromanager.

Working with other people is never easy, but successful managers figure out how to make it happen. You can't be successful if you don't work well with others. Management is getting things done through other people.

Take the time to listen to how your team members perceive you. Take your strengths to the next level and become a more balanced and successful manager. Your success depends on the success of your people. This simple premise will guide your changed behaviour as you become more effective.

Best Practices

1. Ask you peers what type of manager you are.

2. Ask your employees what type of manager you are.

3. Assess your strengths as a manager.

4. Assess your weaknesses as a manager—you already know what they are.

5. Ask your manager to coach you to build on your strengths.

6. Listen more attentively to your people—they do have something to say.

7. Stand up for your people when difficulty strikes—it's a character builder.

8. Get input on important issues and pay attention.

9. Don't look at email when talking to employees—eye contact is good.

10. Empower your people one small step at a time—they won't disappoint.

Chapter 4
The Performance Appraisal

According to the results of a Salary.com survey, as many as 90 percent of performance appraisal processes are inadequate. That is quite a survey result given that most companies, if not all, use some form of performance review. If your company had an area of its business that was 90 percent inadequate, what would you do? I expect you would cut that process loose in a hurry. Why do we hang on to the performance appraisal as if it's some holy grail of management?

Both employees and managers hate the process. It's time consuming for both employees and management, and the results are rarely of any value to either party. It seems our HR friends believe a company needs to rank its employees to discover what everyone knows. Eighty percent of employees are good solid performers, and everyone knows who they are. Ten percent are top performers, and everyone knows who they are. Ten percent are either new or unsuited to the role, and everyone knows who they are. So why do we all go through this agonizing practice of looking back over the previous year to determine the ranking of employees?

Some actually believe the review is an opportunity to discuss performance in detail and gain commitment to new goals for the coming year. Some believe it's an opportunity to motivate employees with an assessment of their performance. Some just need the information for their files. I expect that the last one is the real reason for appraisals. In case we need to terminate someone, we need something in their file. What a sad thought. If this is the real reason, have a look at the files of terminated employees, and you will likely find reviews that don't support the termination. In fact, they're probably rather non-descript when it comes to identifying the true issues. So why do it at all?

I believe it's time for all companies to take a hard look at their performance appraisal process. If regular and consistent coaching is implemented in companies, this annual ritual of appraisals could be eliminated and save millions of dollars in lost productivity. It would also eliminate the two-week anger period after a review, when the office buzz is at its height.

In my research for this book, it became clear that the appraisal performance process simply isn't working as intended. The once-per-year assessment is often biased by the halo effect (see Chapter 10), and the commentary is usually outdated. Let's look at some of the issues regarding the performance-appraisal process that might lead us to revamp the process to make it more effective in assessing true performance and creating effective development objectives for our employees.

It doesn't assess actual performance. Most performance reviews comment on the behaviours rather than the actual results achieved. There are too many subjective comments in a review that miss the intent of assessing performance. High performers are often penalized in their rating due to personal assessments such as being a poor team player or lacking a commitment to the company goals. No one really knows what this means, and these comments cause confusion and irritation.

Infrequent feedback. When a review is completed annually, an employee has little chance to rectify performance throughout the year and must wait for the big hit to arrive at review time. Formal feedback should be delivered through a timely and consistent coaching program like the one outlined in this book. Saving up feedback and bad news is counterproductive when it's dumped on unsuspecting employees once a year. As managers, we know that continual feedback is vital to personal development, so why do we hold back this feedback and let it build up?

Lack of accountability. Managers are not being held accountable for providing accurate feedback. It seems that completing the review is far more important than being accurate. Some managers actually rate a poor performer highly so they can transfer the employee to another division rather than deal with the problem themselves. There is rarely any blowback when this happens, and it happens too often in most companies.

The squeaky wheel gets the oil. The top performers get short shrift on the review process while the poor employee gets the attention. We want to help and spend time finding the right developmental objectives for poor performers while the top performers are left to fend for themselves. What is our payback in overall results when we spend too much time on the poor performers and not enough time on the top performers?

Forced rankings. The famous bell curve is used in most companies to ensure they don't have too many top performers or too many poor performers. Most people will be in the middle. The challenge is that the bell curve is arbitrary. Many of your best performers get downgraded by the bell curve, and they have a hard time understanding why they're rated lower than they expect.

Managers are not trained. Few managers are actually trained on how to assess performance and on how to deliver a performance review. I remember one of my reviews where my manager simply handed me a piece of paper with his commentary on the rating. He said, "Here, read this, and if you have any comments, just note them on the bottom and return it to me." How motivating is this at the one time each year I get to talk about my performance? I'm afraid the process is so complicated and time-consuming that managers don't dedicate the time to completing the review or the time to discuss it in any detail. Many reviews are actually completed by the employee themselves, and the manager just provides the rating, which often bears little resemblance to the narrative provided by the employee. You can see why employees suffer through this annual ritual and are angry for weeks afterward.

Again, a regular coaching program eliminates this demotivating experience and replaces it with positive and constructive feedback to help grow your people.

Managers are biased. I'm sure many of you know the "good guy" manager who is incapable of providing bad news to employees. They avoid confrontation, so they sugar-coat the review with minimal feedback of any value. They also have a tendency to rate high to avoid any confrontation on the rating itself. As a result, most employee ratings end up being the same. HR people know who these easy raters are, but they rarely hold them accountable.

Inconsistency between managers. One of the bigger issues facing companies is the inconsistency of ratings. Some managers are fair, some are tough, and some are soft, and yet each varying performance review and rating are allowed to stand and become part of each employee's ongoing file. This isn't fair to the employees, nor is it fair to other managers who may be interested in transferring employees within the company. These ratings are also important when assessing pay raises and promotions. There is also a huge disparity in writing skills between managers, which again have an impact on an employee's promotability.

I once had a manager who had a flair for words and was able to lay out a precise and compelling case for written reviews. Many details that others didn't include were highlighted. This manager had the best success with promoting employees and was very proud of this accomplishment. I myself was the beneficiary of his word-smith abilities and received a promotion while others with more experience and who were eminently qualified had reviews weak on accomplishments and lacking the detail to support the candidate. Again, companies rarely assess this factor when making employee decisions. The flawed process will haunt organizations until something is done.

Review anxiety. Each year, about a month before review time, employees and managers get anxious about the process. Managers see a lot of work ahead of them, and employees are already starting to fear the performance review because they don't know what's going to happen. If they write their own review, employees ponder for weeks the right words to use and the right results to quantify. Many appraisal forms are long, complicated, and require significant detail that can be up to a year out of date. It's a stressful period for everyone, and we know that productivity declines just before and after the review. If the rating or the comments are less than expected, an employee's anxiety and frustration can last for a month or more after the review. You have to wonder why companies put their people through such an arduous task for so little in return.

What's Next?

I know there is a great vested interest in maintaining this process from all levels of the organization. Notionally, it does make some sense to provide a grade for an individual's performance that can be linked to salary increases and bonuses. The school system has already ingrained in us the need for a grade assessment so we know how we're doing. However, the grades in school are directly related to specific performance on tests while organizations have transferred the need for grades to their companies. They missed the part about tests and in the process have devalued the entire performance review appraisal.

Teachers work with students every day and provide a series of tests and quizzes throughout the year so students know their level of performance on an ongoing basis and can shift their focus to meet their goals. In business, we save up all the marks the "student" has earned on tests during the year and then reveal their results to them all at once and wonder why performance isn't as good as we expected. Can you imagine your son or daughter coming home from school in June with the marks from all their tests throughout the entire year and some commentary about their lack of perform-ance? The student had no idea how they were performing through-out the year but had to wait until the end of school year to see their grades and determine if they passed. As parents, we would demand change, but as managers, we seem to think this process works for companies.

It's time to replace the performance appraisal process with a coaching program that is regular and defined. More on this later in the book. Managers can apply a grade to employees, but there is no need to communicate—communicate the money instead. Use regular coaching to build on strengths and provide feedback and recognition on a regular basis. Save the millions of dollars wasted on annual performance reviews and invest in coaching and training instead. The payback will far exceed your expectations.

Managing Performance Is at the Bottom of the List

This is quite a list of all the things wrong with the performance ap-praisal process. I think you will agree if you honestly look at the value derived from the time and energy expended that there must be a better way to manage performance. I believe we should dis-band the formal performance review as currently used by most companies and replace it with a regular and timely formalized coaching process. The actual notes from coaching sessions can form the basis for performance ratings. There will be no need to deliver an annual review, as each employee will be up to date on performance and progress with each coaching session. No more frustrated manager completing the onerous task of writing and delivering the review. No more frustrated and angry employees upset by bad news. Instead, there will be continual improvement in performance accomplished through a coaching program.

It has been said that completing a performance review program from start to finish costs approximately $2,500 per employee. Do the math. If you have 100 or 1,000 or 10,000 employees, suddenly the cost makes it worth a much closer look. Invest this same money in a coaching plan, and watch the performance of your employees improve over the course of the year compared to what improvements you notice in your current program.

I admit this is a delicate issue, but I do think it's time every company reviewed this time-consuming, confusing, and frustrating review process to determine its true value. If time management is an issue for coaching, then save some time by eliminating the redundant and useless performance review process. Coach, coach, coach!

Best Practices

1. Save big money by eliminating performance appraisals and reinvest it in coaching programs.

2. Eliminate the annual appraisal forms, worksheets, and meetings.

3. Replace the annual performance appraisal process with monthly or bi-weekly coaching based on the criteria outlined in this book.

4. Train all management on coaching skills.

5. Hire interns to assess the effectiveness of your appraisal process and documentation.

6. Set performance metrics that are clear and objective.

7. Focus discussions on the future, not the past.

Chapter 5
Influence in Management

Management is all about changing behaviour to meet the corporate goals. To improve service, employees must behave in a different way that exceeds customer expectations. To improve sales, salespeople must behave in a different way that develops more opportunities and closes more sales. To improve productivity, employees must behave in a different way that is a more efficient use of their time and resources. So what is behaviour? Behaviour is an observable action of what people do and what people say. It's not an attitude but rather outcomes that coaches can readily observe. This is why observation is so critical to the coaching process. Every single hockey coach or basketball coach actually watches the game and reviews game videos so they can observe what players do on the ice or court. Observation is the beginning of the coaching process.

Demanding behavioural change works in the short term, but the costs of monitoring outweighs any benefit. Training will begin the process, but without consistent coaching around the behaviour, the training will dissipate and be replaced with the next training program. The flavour of the day rules most companies, and they wonder why productivity or service suffers and sales goals go unmet. Lasting behavioural change only comes through consistent coaching based on proven principles of influence and persuasion. Sales and marketing have used these principles to good effect to change consumer behaviour. We have the opportunity to use these same principles to change employee behaviour and work with our people to encourage the right pinpointed behaviours that will yield the best results.

There has been significant research over the past sixty years into why people do things. Most managers have not availed themselves of what has been learned. This book will help you apply the best principles of influence.

Self-Fulfilling Prophecy

The concept of the self-fulfilling prophecy is the basis for every behavioural change you may plan to implement. Robert K. Merton coined the term in his book *Social Theory and Social Structure*. The concept is quite simple. Once a prediction is made, the prediction itself actually causes itself to come true. If we believe we will fail, we will automatically put into place activities that will ensure failure. Conversely, if we believe we will succeed, we will put into place activities that will ensure our success.

In management, people will meet our expectations not just because they may want to but also because we will automatically create the environment for them to meet those expectations. This is an amazingly powerful motivational tool to change behaviour if used effectively. Most of the time it happens and we don't even know we are doing it.

Professor Robert Rosenthal published a key study on this philosophy in his book *Pygmalion in the Classroom*. He collected over 300 studies of the self-fulfilling prophecy in action. In classroom experiments, a group of children were divided into two groups. One group was given a teacher who was told that the students were high achievers and should do well. The other teacher was told her students were underachievers who needed help.

At the beginning of the school year, there was no difference between the groups in terms of ability. What do you think happened by the end of the year? The group labelled "high achievers" were doing above-average work. The group labelled "low achievers" were doing below-average work. Why did this happen when the students had the same academic ability? The expectations each teacher had about their class affected their performance with their students. A teacher who believes students are smart will treat the students differently than a teacher who believes the students are below average. This difference in expectation produced totally different results. The students themselves started to believe they were above average or below average based on their teacher's influence, and this led to performance that supported their beliefs.

It can be said that people like people who meet their expectations and that people unconsciously create situations that encourage the expected behaviour. Think of this in terms of your own children. Think of this in terms of your employees and the effect this may have on them. Finally, think of this in terms of yourself and how this can affect your performance. What you expect to come true is usually what you make come true. As Henry Ford said, "If you think you can, you will. If you think you can't, you're right."

All of us have had bosses who we felt showed favouritism to some employees. The reason this happens can generally be placed at the foot of the self-fulfilling prophecy. Managers naturally think employees they like will perform better. They will look for things that support their assessment. You as a manager need to be aware of being susceptible to this same malady. We all are susceptible. Generally, we see favouritism coming from others but rarely coming from ourselves. This may be a little delusional because we all have the tendency to gravitate to those we see as good performers, and then we find more success in them. A word to the wise for every manager: It will happen to you, so try to reassess your objective opinions on a regular basis and don't be tricked.

On the other hand, if you believe your people are good solid performers and you find them doing things right, they will in fact be better performers. This is the real growth formula for managers. We live up to the expectations of ourselves and of others. This is why having objectives and writing them down has such a powerful impact on future behaviour. Setting objectives invokes the self-fulfilling prophecy as we work to make them come true. The psychology is compelling. In discussing the impact of the self-fulfilling prophecy, we will refer to the seven principles of influence and persuasion:

1. Reciprocity
2. Concessions
3. Consensus
4. Authority
5. Scarcity
6. Commitment/consistency
7. Liking

Dr. Robert Cialdini originally highlighted these principles in his book *Influence: The Psychology Persuasion*. I also addressed them in my book *Life Is Sales*.

Reciprocity. We all have a natural tendency to pay back the same form of behaviour that was first given to us. In other words, we feel we have an obligation to reciprocate. It's the principle of exchange, and every single culture in the world teaches its children this basic principle of getting along with others.

In management, this principle can be found in teamwork, where management must find the magic in building and maintaining effective teams. No one can be ordered to be a contributing member of a team; it must come from the individual and the team dynamics. Using this principle effectively smoothes the way for people to work together in unison for superior results.

Concessions. We all have a natural tendency to make a concession to another person if that person has made a concession to us. This means making concessions includes the principle of reciprocity as well. It's the art of negotiation.

All managers must be adept at the art of negotiation to get a consensus on issues and gain commitments from employees on specific goals, targets, or behaviours. Those who know how to negotiate will be far more productive than those who demand compliance.

Consensus. We all have a natural tendency to look at what others are doing to help us determine what we should do. This is particularly powerful when we are unsure of the right thing to do. Managers attempt to clarify priorities for employees, but employees generally have a poor understanding of their company's vision, mission statement, and top priorities, especially when it comes to translating these into actions they're expected to perform. When in doubt, people look to others to decide what the correct behaviour is.

As managers, this presents invaluable opportunities. Consensus building can happen by using top performers as guides to changing behaviour. You will reach a tipping point in behavioural change when employees observe the increasing number of high-performing employees demonstrating the right behaviours. Of course, this also applies when too many demonstrate the wrong behaviour without any direct consequences, including you. Remember, your staff watches you like hawks looking for clues as to how to behave.

Authority. We all have a natural tendency to worship authority figures, and the most powerful authority is a credible authority. Therefore, it's critical that managers recognize the importance of their staff seeing them as an authority. Your staff wants to know two key things about you as a manager: 1) that you are honest, and 2) that you are knowledgeable. Once these two have been established, your authority will be respected and your team will believe what you say and be positively influenced by your requests. Their second-guessing your decisions will diminish, and people will want to move in your direction.

This is not to say that you can now be autocratic, as we can lose this authority component quickly if it's abused. We will discuss in great detail how to build legitimate authority to be more persuasive in getting things done through other people.

Scarcity. We all have a natural tendency to value things that aren't readily available. Scarce items such as diamonds are far more valuable than cubic zirconia gemstones. We all want more of what we can't have. By the same token, we are far more focused on what we will lose than what we will gain. Losing a thousand dollars is far more concerning to us than saving a thousand dollars. The thought of writing a cheque far outweighs the thought of a deposit.

As managers, we can use this principle in ensuring team members truly understand the value proposition of our proposals. We usually explain all the features and benefits of a change we expect to implement and often wonder why people don't jump on the bandwagon and buy into them. Generally, we are fearful of change and usually don't see the true value of the change. If you face resistance when trying to implement a change, simply outline what would happen if you don't implement it. The true impact will become quite clear to your team, and they may respond far more favourably to your proposal because now they realize the value proposition in a completely new way that resonates with them.

Commitment/consistency. We all have a natural tendency to keep our promises once we make them. Once we make a commitment, we all want to keep it. The challenge comes when we try to get a commitment from someone else. This applies both in sales and in management. Most of us prefer to avoid making a commitment because we know that if we make one, we will be obligated to keep it.

Most managers don't get commitments because they don't ask for them. They make statements or commands, and employees don't answer these as they would of something asked of them. If they don't make a commitment, they will be less likely to do anything. Self-established objectives are more effective than imposed objectives.

As managers, how can we get our team members to make commitments? Public commitments are the most powerful, as they invoke several principles of influence at the same time. I have found a simple way to change any statement or command into a question that people will usually say yes to. This is a commitment. Try putting "will you" in front of your usual statement, and then pause and see what happens. These are two magic words that will change behaviour. For example, instead of simply saying, "Submit the report by the end of the day," try asking, "Will you submit the report by the end of the day?" People are more inclined to say yes to the second phrase, and this will solidify a stronger commitment than the first phrase.

Liking. All things being equal, people want to work for someone they like. All things being *unequal*, people still want to work for someone they like. Many managers feel they would sooner be respected than liked; however, few can be respected if they are disliked. The reasons for disliking someone can be quite powerful, and these affect behaviour. If you dislike someone, you probably also don't trust them. Trust is the absolute basis for any successful change in an organization. A great manager should be both respected and liked for all of the right reasons.

What can you do to ensure you are respected as a manager and liked as a person? The propinquity effect describes how people like people they see often. Absentee managers behind closed doors don't even give themselves the opportunity to be liked. Don't forget your team wants to like you, so give them the chance and be proactive in liking them first.

We will delve into each of these principles in future chapters and apply them specifically to the coaching process, exploring concrete practical solutions for a manager to become an effective coach.

Best Practices

1. Be positive about the future.

2. Be positive about the skills of your team members.

3. Be positive about your team's desire to perform.

4. Believe that you can make a difference.

5. Write down your goals and review them weekly.

6. Make sure your goals are behavioural and not just results-oriented.

7. Make the goals achievable.

8. Celebrate small wins often on your journey to big wins.

9. Find what is right about things and build on that.

10. "If it's to be, it's up to me"—take ownership of your life and career.

Chapter 6
The Rule for Reciprocity

Connie Bird tells this story in our book *Life Is Sales*.

The day after we moved into our country home, a neighbour knocked on our door. Kathy refused to step into the disarray. From the porch, she welcomed us to the area and insisted we come over to her house for coffee when we were ready to take a break. We accepted her invitation and enjoyed our first visit with our new neighbours.

Kathy and Gord told stories about the masons who put up our beautiful stonework, about the eighteen-foot snow-drifts, mice, and houseflies. By the end of our visit, the differences between country and subdivision living were growing apparent. We were most appreciative of their hospitality and their country living lessons. As we turned to leave, I was compelled to reciprocate, as though some spirit moved into my body and took over my mouth. There was absolutely no choice in the matter; it just spilled from my lips: "Will you come over to our house next?" The need to repay Kathy and Gord for their kindness was overpowering me.

That need to repay weighed heavily until we were

finally ready to have Gord and Kathy to the Bird abode for a visit. Why did I feel so compelled to repay an invitation to a virtual stranger?

Maybe it was the time you arrived at the entrance of a department store at the same time as another shopper. The shopper opened the door and gestured for you to go in. You smiled, bowed your head in thanks, and stepped in quickly. You automatically opened the second door, gestured with your hand and a smile for him to proceed this time. And you felt relieved when he did, as your brief debt was repaid. The stranger's kind gesture was repaid all in a matter of seconds with a like gesture. Why do we do this?

When I invite you to dinner at my house, you will probably invite me to dinner at your house next. If a friend buys you a coffee on break today, will you buy her one on break tomorrow? If you do me a favour, I owe you a favour in return. We create a sense of obligation in others by giving something. What is this feeling we have that makes us respond this way?

In our quest to develop management skills, we will look at the Rule for Reciprocity. In his book *Influence: The Psychology of Persuasion*, Dr. Robert Cialdini goes so far as to say that this human phenomenon is a "universal principle" and calls it a manager's dream. This principle applies every day and everywhere in life. In fact, humans have been automatically responding this way for thousands of years.

Simply stated, the Rule for Reciprocity says, "I am obligated to give back to you the form of behaviour that was first given to me." When someone does something for us or gives us something, we feel obligated to do something for that person in return. Most of us try to be fair and equitable in our life. The Rule for Reciprocity is sometimes referred to as "the principle of exchange," and it and has ruled the economies of the world for centuries. Every single culture teaches its children this basic rule of exchange. "Be sure to give in return for what you have taken." "Please share; you'll feel bad if you don't."

"Say thank you when someone gives you something." These are all things we say to our children. That sense of obligation has formed the basis of our cultural heritage, and we start teaching it to our children at a very young age. Our ancestors set the groundwork for reciprocity as they exchanged services for services, and commodities for commodities. Barter was the medium of exchange, and if someone gave a product away, it was assumed that it would be repaid at a later date. Fast forward to the twenty-first century. What do we do today? In many impersonal transactions, we use money as a means for valuing our exchange of goods and services. We pick up a loaf of bread at the store and have an obligation to pay for that loaf of bread. Barter systems and referral networks are commonplace, and their roots are based in the Rule for Reciprocity. As you grow aware of this automatic human response, you will learn to intentionally create it in others so they feel compelled to help you.

In the context of obligation and management, people will say yes to your requests more often if they feel they owe you something as a result of your giving them something previously. This will get far more cooperation in the workplace, better teamwork on individual teams, and better relationships between teams in different work silos (which tend to operate as disparate systems and have difficulty with external reciprocity).

In this chapter, you will learn how to create and recognize priceless moments of opportunity to help you create a positive and cooperative work environment. You will learn how to optimize these moments to better capitalize on what is already yours. You will learn how to make powerful requests and improve your results.

Reciprocity in Action

Our fundamental need to repay others seems pretty simple. Giving creates a sense of obligation in the receiver. Professor Harrison, a university professor in Santa Barbara, California, decided one Christmas season to send greeting cards to a sample of perfect strangers. He went to phone books and picked out a random sample of people in various cities across the United States and sent these people a Christmas card. He anticipated some kind of response from these cards but was not prepared for the avalanche of cards he received from these absolute strangers. It seemed that people received a card from this professor and simply sent a card back without question. It was an automatic response to repay in kind for the gift they had just received. It's this automatic response that we are most interested in when it comes to being more persuasive and influential.

In his video program *The Power of Persuasion*, Cialdini takes this Christmas card story even further. He apparently told the Christmas card story to one of his classes at the University of   Arizona. One year a student came up to him after class to talk about it. She was a mature student who had already raised her family and had decided to return to school. She told Cialdini that he had just solved a decade-long mystery in her home. She had received a Christmas card about ten years ago from the Harrisons in California, and she didn't know any Harrisons. She had asked her husband, but he didn't know any Harrisons, and her kids were too young at the time, so with a great deal of effort, she resisted sending them a card that year because she thought it was a mistake. But the following year, they had recieved another card from the Harrisons, so she sent them a card. They were now in the tenth year of exchanging cards with these people, and she still didn't know who they were.

The rest of story is equally amazing. This woman sent Cialdini an email saying her son had been accepted into all the colleges he had applied to, including his top choice, the University of California in Santa Barbara. He was such a good student that he was invited to attend the honours convocation. It was to occur one day before the university opened, so his dorm room wasn't ready, and he needed a place to stay in Santa Barbara. She thought, "Who do we know in Santa Barbara?" The Harrisons of course. So she phoned him. Now, she didn't just send a card; she included a photocopy of all the details of what happened in their life the past year—photos, the works. And what did Professor Harrison say when she asked if her son could stay with them? He said of course he could, because they have known him for years.

Now should the Harrisons have a son or daughter travelling across the U.S. who needs a place to stay in Arizona, then the woman and her family should open their doors in welcome. And why not? It's a perfect system of exchange, and this is the same power behind reciprocity in the field of management. The principle of exchange has been around since the dawn of time and has kept humanity in good stead, but now professional managers can and should use this tool to build bridges between teams and inspire employees to work more effectively with each other.

In 1985, a country provided financial aid to Mexico, which had experienced a severe 8.0 magnitude earthquake. We feel compelled to give to those countries that are in desperate need, especially in times of natural disasters. However, the money in this instance came from Ethiopia, a poor Third World country whose people suffer horribly from disease and starvation. This didn't make sense! Shouldn't the money have gone from Mexico to Ethiopia? Ethiopia was appealing to the world for food and support for their own people, and here they were giving aid to Mexico! Even though Ethiopia had a desperate need for food, shelter, and clothing for their own population, the Ethiopian Red Cross sent $5,000 to Mexico City. When asked why a country in such a desolate state would feel compelled to give to another, the Ethiopian Red Cross said they sent the money because Mexico helped them in 1935, when Italy invaded Ethiopia. This was repayment of a long past debt. Fifty years later, the sense of obligation remained strong. Catastrophic suffering from dire conditions of disease, famine, and cultural differences didn't dissuade Ethiopia to give back to Mexico. Once Ethiopia was aware of an opportunity to repay their obligation to the country that had given them such a wondrous gift fifty years prior, they did so and proudly. Large favours are remembered for a long time. This is the Rule for Reciprocity at work in the world.

A Gift Improves Results

Psychologist Dennis Regan created a classic study of reciprocity, which he published in "Effects of a favor and liking on compliance" in the *Journal of Experimental Psychology*. He had subjects work in pairs in a fake art appreciation study. One of the subjects was an actor, and during a short recess, the actor would leave the group. For one set of groups, he would return with a Coke for his partner, and in the other groups, he would return with no gift at all. In both situations, the actor would ask the participants for a favour. He was selling raffle tickets for his high school back home, and he would receive a prize if he sold the most raffle tickets. He asked the participants if they would be willing to buy one of his raffle tickets. The results were surprising. The actor sold almost twice as many tickets to the groups of people who had received the free Coke.

It would appear that the participants had a sense of obligation to repay the actor for the free beverage. When he asked them to buy something, this group was more likely to say yes to his request. The actor used reciprocity to create an environment for increased sales.

In another part of the study, Regan varied the likeability of the actor. He wanted to determine if people are more willing to do favours for people they like. In this case, the actor had to answer the phone, and in half of the groups, he was extremely rude to a customer on the phone. The other half witnessed the actor being quite polite on the phone instead. The results, as expected, were that the actor sold more of his raffle tickets when he was pleasant and polite on the phone. However, the importance of the likeability factor was no match for the unsolicited bottle of free Coke. The free beverage almost doubled the sales compared to only a 20 percent reduction in sales when he acted rude on the phone. The interesting aspect was that the free beverage had as much effect on ticket sales when he was rude as when he was polite. The free beverage trumped the likeability factor, so it didn't matter if they liked him or not. It was far more important that they had a sense of owing the actor something in return for the gift he had just given them, and so they bought more raffle tickets.

Shoppers at Costco are familiar with the Rule for Reciprocity at work. Tasty samples of food are given away free at the end of every other aisle! When you try a sample, don't you feel just a little guilty if you don't buy the product? (Especially if you liked it.) Maybe you take the product, faking interest in buying it, and return it to the shelf later, or maybe you fake a compliment in exchange for the sample. This is where I lunch on Saturdays—the free sample counters at Costco! If I don't buy the product, I do feel compelled to comment about it to the employee.

Teamwork

To see how all this works in the realm of management, let me tell about one of my own experiences. I was working with a mortgage company a few years ago, and there seemed to be a rift between the salespeople and the underwriters. The salespeople wanted every mortgage application approved, but the underwriters didn't trust the brokers, so they were extremely conservative in their underwriting. The salespeople would get angry with the underwriters, accusing them of sabotaging their deals, and the underwriters became even harder to deal with. This ugly relationship started to affect customer service, and sales volumes were suffering. What could management do to rebuild the trust and regain their market share?

They tried appealing to the logic of working together, but this had little impact. They tried a team-building exercise, which only erupted into angry accusations on both sides. I suggested they try the principle of reciprocity to mend the fence and get the two sides working together for the betterment of both teams. They both knew they needed each other to be successful. They even knew that if they didn't fix it, people could lose their jobs, but that wasn't enough to change behaviour. A manager had to lead the way.

We tried a series of gifts to see if reciprocity would result in changing behaviour. Every time a deal was approved, the salesperson would phone the underwriter and thank them for doing a thorough job and helping the client get into the home of their dreams. The sales manager monitored this carefully at first to ensure no sarcasm sneaked into the discussions.

The manager of the sales group bought big bags of licorice, and every week, he would go around to the individual underwriter's desk and offer a licorice. The underwriters felt compelled to return the favours and actually started to call salespeople to thank them for complete applications. Completeness on the applications helped them speed up the approval process for the clients. The licorice became a conversation piece amongst the underwriters, and comments about the salespeople not being so bad started to circulate. Within two months, the service levels had improved significantly, clients were happier, and approval rates increased. Underwriters started to call salespeople with questions rather than simply bouncing the deals back, which is what they used to do.

Overall, an amazing shift occurred in two separate teams with the introduction of gifts of compliments and licorice. It's hard to believe that a simple gift of a licorice could have such a profound impact on human behaviour, but that's the power of reciprocity.

So why did such a simple plan well executed have such a powerful impact in such a short time? The Rule of Reciprocity ruled the day. The underwriters really had no choice but to give back to the salespeople who had given to them. And once the underwriters started to give to the salespeople, the salespeople had no choice but to give back as well. It snowballed in a matter of months to change the working environment. This is what great managers do: find the simple solutions to tough problems and ensure an effective implementation. The vision of the company played no role in changing behaviour. It was the actions of the committed and detailed manager and the people who started the whole process.

Can you imagine what the executives of the company would

have said if the manager told them he was going to solve the relationship crisis with a licorice and a compliment? This is why executives lead but managers execute.

Making Requests

It's one thing to order people to do things; it's another thing entirely to make requests. If giving gifts isn't practical in your situation, being in a position to make powerful requests can be just as effective. For example, in Peterborough, one of my workshop clients shared her frustration in making a request of her young child. She hated the cold snowy winter months because of the extra work in getting her son dressed in his snowsuit and boots. I asked her what she said to her son as they got ready to leave the house. She replied, "Get your snowsuit on! Do it now! Stop fooling around!" She stopped. She heard the words as they came out of her mouth. She was even a tad embarrassed as she shared in front of her peers. She gave an order, and never actually made a request of her child. It would take over ten minutes of nagging and complaining to get her son dressed, so she was willing to practice making a powerful request.

She wrote me back a few days after the workshop. "I'm shocked it works." She said she tried it out the next day. She called out sweetly to her son, "Honey, will you do Mommy a favour?"

"Sure, Mommy," her son replied.

"Will you please put on your snowsuit?"

"Sure, Mommy."

The morning battles were a thing of the past. Here we have a powerful request in action. Managers can use this same technique in making requests with their employees. When trying to implement change, gifts are an effective tool; however, knowing how to make requests that encourage results is important as well.

Why Go First?

If there is someone you want to influence, how will you proceed? You want to be a master of influence; you need to take control of the situation. How will you accomplish this?

It's up to you to go first. Don't wait for someone else to set the tone for the relationship you want to have. A good mantra to have in management is, "Give first, give first, give first." A thoughtful gift will get the thanks you are after, so jump into this moment of opportunity with both feet.

As a manager, you need to take the initiative in motivating your team. Taking initiative is how to make things happen. When you move into a new home in a new neighbourhood and want to make friends, what do you do? You don't sit in the backyard with a few beers and wait; you may be waiting a long time. No. You invite your neighbours to your house. Even if they find out they don't like you much, they will feel obligated to invite you back to their house and the relationship will begin. It's the same with management. If you want a better relationship with another team, find a way to give first and the relationship will blossom.

Employees who don't seem engaged in their job need this kind of boost in the relationship. Money isn't the only way to motivate people, and it's not even the most effective. Allowing staff to participate is an amazing gift, and the gift of empowerment will motivate people to be more creative and engaged in their job.

When addressing a group, I have found that giving the gift of information not readily available to the staff makes people want to share more in return and feel more a part of the company. Sharing "secrets" or eliminating the need-to-know basis of sharing will do wonders for team engagement and loyalty to the organization. Few managers appreciate the power of sharing information. Most employees are hungry for information on where they're going. If you're more open, they will be more open with each other. The benefits are astounding, and it's all free!

Start with Why

In his book *Start with Why*, Simon Sinek explores the power of employees when they know the why of their company. Most leaders and managers feel their employees only have to know what to do and how to do it to be successful. These managers make the tragic mistake of believing that only the management needs to know why people in the company do things. These managers share information on a need-to-know basis and keep employees in the dark as to even why the company is in business. However, when employees know why, they suddenly feel a part of something bigger than themselves and automatically become more engaged. Sinek provides many examples and stories that highlight the power of employees when they understand why.

The why of a company is the perfect gift for managers to share with employees. When they know why their contributions matter, employees feel they are on the inside and better understand the company and its goals. When they receive this gift, they must reciprocate by understanding the why and implementing the why into all of their decisions. This is the real power behind successful companies. Decisions and actions shift when everyone knows why they do things rather than just how to do things. Creative new ideas to accomplish the why come to the fore when everyone is on the same page.

People will challenge the status quo when they know the why, and managers will inspire when they know the why. Too many of us focus on the what and the how. If you don't know the why, it's time to ask.

Gift vs. Reward

Managers generally feel that incentive programs are effective in guiding the behaviour of employees. Money, after all, is a motivator, and most companies have some form of incentive program from bonuses to trips to salary increases. But is a gift or a reward more effective in getting the behaviour you want? Which works better? Giving employees a gift beforehand or giving a reward as a result of their actions? Do incentives work better than gifts?

Let's look to a survey campaign outlined in Robert Cialdini's *Power of Persuasion* presentation in which the two techniques were employed. The survey organizers gifted a $20 cheque to one group of professionals and followed up with a request to complete their lengthy survey. They promised a $20 cheque to a second group of professionals if they completed the survey. Sixty-six percent of the professionals who were promised a cheque as a reward for their time responded to the survey. Seventy-eight percent of the professionals who were given a gift of $20 in advance responded. For the curious, a mere 1 percent of the professionals cashed the gift cheque and didn't return the completed survey. The results show what we have learned: a gift followed by a request gets a noticeable improvement in response rates.

Money is rarely a motivator, but the lack of money is definitely a demotivator. A bonus provides about two weeks of joy for employees before they convince themselves that they deserved it in the first place and go back to normal. However, a gift develops an obligation to repay it and invokes the principle of reciprocity, which is the basis for teamwork.

I have tried a few experiments with servers in restaurants. Most of us provide a tip at the end of the meal as a reward for good service. Try giving your tip first and see if you get a different level of service. In every instance that I provided a cash tip in advance, the service level skyrocketed and the server was all over us with exceptional attention to our needs. I have even received a free sampler of an appetizer. Each time, the server just felt compelled to reciprocate.

So how can we as managers use this natural human response in our business of getting things done through other people? Be creative in finding ways to give to your people. One extremely successful gift is a compliment immediately after an accomplishment. This may well be a surprise, but to make it effective, it must be specific to the behaviour and it must be a behaviour you want to encourage. A phrase such as "good job" is pointless. Be specific. For example: "I like the way you demonstrated initiative by resolving that customer complaint so quickly. You accepted the fact we made an error, apologized, and delivered the replacement immediately. That's our customer service philosophy, and you demonstrated it beautifully." If you find ways for teams to cooperate more effectively through sharing, it will become the norm. Give your people empowerment and they will become empowered. Micromanage your people and they will be micromanagers too, which will defeat all your efforts for creativity and service excellence. Show your people respect and they will respect your customers. It seems almost too simple, but often the simplest answer is the right one. Try it on and see what happens. Give the tip first and you may be surprised with the result.

The best gifts are personal and a surprise. Make them count!

Responding to Thank You

A response of thanks after receiving a gift is just as important as gift giving itself. We all have a natural tendency to downplay the gift we give, and when someone says thank you, we often respond with "no problem." What does "no problem" really mean? It downplays the significance of your efforts, so it diminishes the power of reciprocity and the recipient will feel no need to repay anything. Saying "no problem" defeats the purpose of the gift in the first place. Most of us do use "no problem" far too often, and we're missing out on that opportunity to change behaviour.

So what can you say? I suggest you build on the sense of obligation so that people will feel more obliged to pay you back and agree to your request. Some examples include:

- "It was my pleasure to recognize your contribution. I know you are a true team player and that we will build a better relationship with our customers."

- "This is just what good business partners do for each other."
- "If the situation were ever reversed, I know you would do the same for me."

Find the words that work best for you. Write them down and even practice how you would deliver them. A thank you is a critical moment of opportunity for every manager to build relationships and trust between employees and management, between employees and their team, and between teams.

Best Practices

1. **Practice flexing your reciprocity muscles.**

2. **Learn the why of your company and share it with your team.**

3. **Decide whom you want to influence—you are the initiator in building relationships to new levels.**

4. **Decide on a thoughtful gift or favour to give to your employees—make it personal and a surprise.**

5. **Carefully script what you will say after the recipient says thank you.**

6. **Give first, give first, give first and create that moment of opportunity.**

7. **Make your response to a thank you come from the heart.**

8. **Smile and look the employee in the eye when you deliver your response.**

9. **Pause for a few seconds after your response to let the sense of obligation sink in, and then ask them for what you want.**

Chapter 7
The Principle of
Concessions

Concessions are a part of reciprocity. It's at the core of the art of negotiating. If someone makes a request and you say no, then the requester has the option of making a concession. If a concession is made, you will be inclined to say yes to the concession because you will feel a certain obligation to give something back.

This is a natural tendency we all have. It happened to me a number of years ago. I was at the local mall, and at the entrance was a Boy Scout selling tickets to a music jamboree. As I approached the doors, this twelve-year-old boy said, "Excuse me, sir. I'm selling tickets to the Boy Scout music jamboree this weekend. The tickets are only twenty dollars apiece. Would you like to buy two tickets?"

I said, "No. I won't be home this weekend," and started to walk away.

Before I could escape, the boy said, "Well, if you can't do that, would you be willing to buy a couple of my chocolate bars here? They're only two dollars apiece."

I immediately reached into my pocket and handed the boy $4 and walked away with two chocolate bars. I stopped in the middle of the hall, looked at the chocolate bars, and realized that something significant had just happened. He had managed to persuade me to buy two chocolate bars when I didn't want any. I don't even like chocolate.

Why did this work so effectively? The boy had made the larger request worth $40, and I said no. When he made a concession worth $4, however, I felt obliged to make a concession in return, so I did. Will this simple philosophy work in changing behaviour in your workplace? Is this really so powerful that people will agree to your concessions?

As managers, our natural tendency is to make small requests because we don't want to deal with the negativity of someone saying no. We should, however, make requests as large as we want them to be. If a request is refused, we only need to make a concession to gain compliance.

The Negotiation

The key to good negotiating with employees is to know what you want first and then simply ask for it. You should know what you want because you just may get it right away, so go big and be prepared to negotiate. In his classic book *Seven Habits of Highly Effective People,* Stephen R. Covey puts it this way: "Begin with the end in mind." Create your desired outcome, and you will be more likely to accomplish it.

One of my favourite stories I have heard when presenting my workshop "The Power of Persuasion" came from a young mother who was having trouble getting her young son to clean his room. I expect many other parents have experienced this as well. She had tried several techniques to no avail. She had bribed him with the offer of an iPod touch if he kept the room clean for two weeks. He made it only two days. Incentives don't work to change behaviour. She tried punishing him by taking away his video games, but that resulted in horrible behaviour. She even begged to no avail. Finally, she just closed the door and let the mess accumulate, but it bothered her a great deal.

At our training workshop, she asked, "What can I try now? Nothing has worked, and I'm at my wit's end with him."

Apparently, the young boy was a good kid in all other aspects.

He was a good student, didn't get into much trouble, and was generally quite polite. He was only eight years old, so I told his mother to try an approach that invokes the principle of commitment tied with concessions.

I said to her, "Next Saturday, tell your son that you have some work to do together. Say these words to him: 'Will you clean your room, clean the bathroom, and vacuum the family room today before ten-thirty?' When he says no, make a concession." I told her to use the technique the young Boy Scout used on me. I told her to say, "Well, if you can't do all that, will you clean your room today?"

She didn't think it would work, but she would try it. The following week, I received a phone call from her, and she was astounded. The request had worked; he had actually cleaned his room. When the young boy had said no, his mother had made a concession and he felt obligated to make a concession in return. So he agreed to her concession.

I then told her that this will work for a while, but sooner or later, he will figure out what she's doing. We hoped by then he will discover that a clean room is far nicer to live in than a messy one.

Objectives

Setting objectives with people is usually a time-consuming and frustrating experience. I remember sitting with a management team and negotiating budgets with the executive. We called it a bun-throwing competition, as everyone had a vested interest in getting a larger budget while the executives were committed to reducing expenses. The discussions usually got quite heated as individuals tried to showcase why they needed the budget while their fellow managers didn't. We would lob fictional buns at each other to discredit the others' arguments and augment ours.

This was not conducive to teamwork by any means, but in the end, with some executive dictates, we did manage to work out the budget arrangements. Many of us were using the principle of concessions without realizing the psychology behind the approach.

We would go in high because we knew we would get cut. If some-one came in at a reasonable number, they too would get cut. Some-times the executives would apply a standard cut to everyone, and those who were reasonable got penalized. In other words, the ne-gotiations were set up to encourage all of us to highball our pro-jections to protect against a standard reduction for everyone. It's not really an effective way to gain commitments to objectives.

When negotiating with your people on service, sales, or budget targets, don't fall into the trap that the executives fell into. Be fair and outline what the corporate situation is. These numbers are usu-ally top-down directives. You are now negotiating with individuals on your team. By using a regular coaching system, you can estab-lish short-term goals with the big annual goal in mind. If you make a concession to them on the objective, they will be more likely to make a concession to you and agree to the commitment. The agree-ment part is crucial. If it's their objective, they will be more diligent in attaining it than if you arbitrarily set the objective yourself.

I have seen too many salespeople complain for months on end about objectives that seem impossible to attain, and it drives the enthusiasm right out of the group. If they believe they will fail, they probably will. But if they feel they have skin in the game and the numbers are theirs and are achievable, they will move heaven and earth to achieve them.

Negotiate First

Those who negotiate first usually win. If you lay out the department objectives so the employees get a feel for the lay of the land, their numbers will usually be better than if they start completely from their own perspectives. Once you establish the big number, each person can take a piece, and the numbers can be negotiated down using concessions. This is a delicate exercise, I agree, but if done properly, it will generate a true commitment to achieve the objec-tives of the group.

Tardiness

Joseph (not his real name) was an employee of mine who was habitually late for work. I had tried all the usual approaches of discipline, reprimands, and logic and tried to understand why but all to no avail. I would make progress only to have the habit return shortly thereafter. Finally, I arranged a meeting with Joseph to try something new. I explained that tardiness was unacceptable behaviour in the organization and I could no longer tolerate it. His hours were from 8 a.m. to 4 p.m., but he usually arrived around 9 or 9:30 a.m. He always worked late, however, and got all of his work done up to standard and beyond. He did good work. The only performance issue was the tardiness.

I sat Joseph down and told him we were changing his hours from 11 a.m. to 7 p.m. to eliminate the fact that he was always late. I stated that he was a valuable employee and did excellent work but the tardiness was unacceptable. He was surprised with the offer to work different hours and said he just couldn't stay until 7 p.m. every day because of his personal life. So I told him if he couldn't do those hours, he could work 9 to 5 every day. Joseph smiled and said he could certainly be there for 9 a.m. every single day, and he was from that point onward. He made a fresh commitment based on the principle of concession, and he kept his promise. His work actually improved, and the rest of the team became supportive by focusing on his new schedule rather than focusing on the fact he was always late.

Deal with the Elephant

Every manager is judged by how they handle the elephant in the room. If you don't deal with problem situations, then the uninvolved employees may think that this is proper behaviour even though they know it isn't. You will lose respect if you ignore the problem child in your office. By ignoring the tardy worker, you tell your people that being on time isn't important. By ignoring the rude staff member, you condone rude behaviour in your department. By allowing poor customer service by one employee, you indicate to everyone that customer service isn't a priority.

Employees will watch your every move to determine how to behave. You can use the principle of concessions to influence behavioural and attitudinal change and get your team back on track. Make the big request but be ready to make a concession to win the day.

Best Practices

1. **Make more powerful requests.**

2. **Wait for employees to say yes—be patient.**

3. **Showcase to your team what is important—actions speak volumes.**

4. **Be fair but firm.**

5. **Aim for achievable objectives rather than unobtainable ones— people will overachieve realistic objectives.**

6. **Offer people concessions to gain a commitment from them.**

7. **Negotiate first.**

8. **Deal with the elephant in the room.**

Chapter 8
Commitment/ Consistency

We all have a natural tendency to want harmony in our lives. We like things to be predictable. Surprises are a nice change of pace, but if our whole life were full of surprises, the stress load would be enormous. We like a degree of consistency in our life. This is part of the reason why change management is so tough.

We like to know we have a job, and we like to think we have job security. We generally perform better if we are comfortable in our jobs. We have habits that are a part of our being. We drive to work the same way most of the time because it's familiar. We drink the same soft drinks, eat the same snacks, and keep the same friends in our life. We want consistency. With this drive for consistency influencing our decisions, it can be concluded that we also need to be consistent when we make a commitment. When we make a promise, we all want and need to keep that promise to maintain our internal harmony. There are rather severe social consequences for those who don't keep their promises. These people are called liars, welchers, moochers, and other terms that indicate their unreliability. We all like to think that we can be trusted to keep our word, and this drives us to be consistent with our promises. This tendency we all have can be a powerful management tool in getting things done.

We Expect Consistency

Life must make sense to us, and when it doesn't, we must expend energy to try to resolve this inconsistency. We actually expect consistency in our lives. When we flip a light switch, we expect the light bulb to turn on. If it doesn't, we experience some minor stress as we realize something is wrong. We want things to work the same way every time they happen. When we turn the ignition key in our car, we expect the engine to turn over and start every single time. What would your life look like if you never knew if your car would start every time you turned the ignition? Your stress level would escalate each time you sat in the car and put the key in as you wondered if it would start today. You wouldn't live with this situation for long. Your solution would be to find a consistency missing in your life and eliminate this unpredictable situation. You would buy another car that was reliable.

We expect consistency in the physical world, be we also expect it in the psychological world. We expect our relationships to be intact when we wake every morning, and we expect it to be much the same as it was when we went to bed. This may be good or bad depending on the circumstances, but we do expect it to be much the same. We expect the attitudes of our spouses, friends, and co-workers to be much the same as it was yesterday. When mood swings enter the picture, we get confused and have difficulty managing the situation because the behaviour is inconsistent with what we expect. Our expectation for consistency in others is complemented by our own personal need for consistency in ourselves. This need for consistency is natural, and it helps brings stability and harmony to all of our lives.

Inconsistencies

Life sometimes deals us unexpected cards, which may disturb our harmony. We know things don't always work out as planned, and sometimes things hit us in surprising and unexpected ways. This creates an inconsistency between what we expect and what we experience. It's your birthday—you expected a gift from your family, but everyone forgot. It's Christmas—you expected a surprise gift that would demonstrate some personal thought behind the gift, but instead you get a gift card to The Home Depot. It's performance review time at work—your review is worse than expected and your raise is half of what you were hoping for. You love your job and respect your boss, and you believe you have done an exceptional job, but the review outcome caught you by surprise. How do you feel about these situations? Your natural harmony is disturbed by how you react to these actions that are inconsistent with your expectations.

You believe your job performance was as good if not better than last year, and yet your likeable boss has just rated you poorly. The immediate reaction is confusion. This result is outside your comfort zone, and so you question what really happened and how it could happen. Soon, a mild form of anger moves into your body as your stress level rises. Your heart rate escalates, your hands get sweaty, your face gets flushed, and your mind races as you seek reasons or justification or blame. A defensive response usually appears just after anger, as we all feel the need to defend ourselves from unjustified attacks on our performance and character. Is your job at risk? What did you do wrong? Maybe the boss you used to like is not so good after all. Confusion, anger, and stress all combine to undermine the harmony you once enjoyed. It's very uncomfortable, and it triggers a strong desire to return to a state of harmony.

We all wish to avoid this state at all costs. When we find ourselves experiencing it, we wish to get out of it as soon as possible.

Consistency

Falling from a state of harmony can be an uncomfortable experience. No one can survive this state for long without risking heart disease or other serious health problems, so the desire to regain consistency in our lives is overpowering. We all must deal with dissonance and get rid of it as soon as possible. This is not an easy task, as the self-talk that goes on in our heads can be quite judge-mental. We always engage in self-talk, and it quite often supports the dissonance in our minds by raising all kinds of doubts about our ability to regain harmony. The fear of disruption in our lives travels like waves through both mind and body. Stress escalates and compounds the inconsistency between what happens and what we want. What can we do to regain our harmony?

There are many different ways to deal with these inconsisten-cies in life. The key to remember when it comes to influence is that most people are compelled to eliminate dissonance and restore har-mony and consistency in their lives. Understanding this drive is a powerful tool in the manager's toolkit.

If we make a promise or make a decision, we all need to act consistent with our commitment. We all want to keep our word. Getting a commitment from someone is almost a guarantee that they will keep their promise. If they don't, they will be uncomfort-able with the outcome. A powerful management strategy is to gain a commitment from employees first. A volunteered commitment is effective, but a written commitment is even more effective. We all have a tendency to live up to what we write down.

Changing Minds

Is it possible to get someone to do something they don't believe in? Is it possible to have people behave counter to their true atti-tudes? How can we change attitudes to obtain the behaviour we're looking for? In management, there is a major opportunity to change people's attitudes. Changing attitudes and behaviour are important in our quest for continual improvement.

A common research method to prove this point has been used countless times. First, a researcher would survey people's opinion on some topic that is against their true views, say, capital punish-ment or welfare programs. One group would be forced to write an essay contrary to their views as a requirement for their educational credit while another group would be asked to volunteer to write the essay. Both groups were surveyed again on their opinions on the topic after they completed the essay.

The group that was forced to participate showed almost no change in their attitudes toward the topic notwithstanding their essay being against their normally held views. They were able to rationalize their essay as being forced and therefore didn't change their opinions on the topic. The volunteer group, however, did register a change in their opinions after they wrote their essay. They volunteered to write an essay that was inconsistent with their previously held views and it was uncomfortable for them. They needed to remove this inconsistency to regain their harmony of thought. The way many of them did this was to change their opinion on the topic to give an alternative view some credence.

The effect of this exercise was differentiated by each essay writer's ability or inability to find an external source to justify their actions. An external source such as a requirement didn't affect an attitude change, but volunteering did.

To regain harmony, if we can't rationalize why we must do something that makes us uncomfortable, we have a tendency to change our beliefs to allow us to remove any discomfort we have in doing it. In managing people, it's important to get commitments as something voluntary rather than forced. This is the difference between an autocratic style of managing and a style that is more influential and persuasive.

How to Manage

How can a manager effectively use what we know about human behaviour to shift the attitudes and even culture of a company? People who volunteer will have some skin in the game and will perform and behave differently from those who are simply told to do something. Setting objectives for individuals or departments is always a challenge for the participants. Implementing a major change in the way we do business is also a major challenge. Many executives try to gain a buy-in from the employees by explaining how important the targets are or how vital the changes are to the company. Most employees will agree but won't have volunteered to support them. This is why change management is so difficult and setting objectives is so ugly. Individuals who merely agree to the justifications for targets or change may instead set the rumour mill on fire and unintentionally sabotage the efforts of management.

When I was in sales, I accepted the corporate goals for my division but didn't impose these restrictions on the employees. Instead, I asked each individual to set their own targets after they had seen what the company expected us to accomplish as a team. I didn't suggest any numbers but merely asked each of them to review their markets and the competition and provide their own personal objectives for the year. We would then sit in a room together and everyone would share their objectives with the rest of the team. It was interesting to note that when I would add up the individual objectives, the group total would always exceed the company target set by head office. Everybody had volunteered their own targets and was therefore much more committed to them than any targets I would have otherwise imposed on them.

The group would then review all the targets. They would shame the low-ball target setters into accepting higher targets, while the overly optimistic would lower theirs to something more achievable. At the end of the discussions, we would have personally committed to individual objectives and as a team have committed to exceeding the company's targets. This ensured no complaints about targets, which is rampant in most companies. It also eliminated discussions on how the company targets weren't possible. These were replaced with discussions on how we could achieve them. The attitude was totally different than it had been in previous years when targets were imposed with a so-called sales buy-in approach.

Granted, I always received flack from head office about this approach, but I did it anyway. I was convinced that this was a far better way to achieve results than top-down dictums. The results after year-end were always the same: objectives exceeded by handsome margins. It really doesn't matter if the individual totals match the corporate goal or not, as some will always overachieve and some will always underachieve. My objective was to have a commitment to reasonable objectives so that most would be in a position to overachieve. Many executives are attached to hard mathematics and believe that all secondary objectives must add up to the corporate objective. I suggest it doesn't really matter unless the numbers are way off the corporate target.

We all must learn to change behaviours to suit our goals to get the results we want. Do the right thing, the right way, and you will get the right results. Focusing exclusively on results, however, undermines the need for behavioural coaching. The key is to involve your people in the decision-making process, but make sure they have some power and that it's not just window dressing. They are, after all, the ones who will get the job done.

Incentives

Will incentives cause people to change their minds on certain issues? Certainly many marketing companies and sales organizations strongly believe in incentives, but what does the research say?

In the study mentioned above regarding the essay that was either voluntary or non-voluntary, they added another stimulus. Half the essay writers were given an incentive of $20 to write the essay that was counter to their beliefs. The other half was given a $0.50 payment to write the essay. This is a significant difference in incentives. Which group do you think experienced an attitudinal change after the essay was written?

The results were surprising. The group that was paid $20 showed very little change in their attitudes while the group paid $0.50 displayed significant changes in their attitudes. Why did this happen?

Both groups in this study were volunteers and agreed to write an essay that was counter to their beliefs. During the exercise, they experienced cognitive dissonance, as they wrote from a position inconsistent with their own beliefs. The group that was paid $20 for this essay could justify writing the material because they were paid for it. They could therefore remain consistent with their views because they had been paid to act otherwise. They did it for the money, and this was enough to regain harmony in their minds, and they could comfortably retain their previous attitudes. Justification was at work in dealing with the inconsistent behaviour. The $20 payment actually forced them to write the essay, and so the dissonance simply disappeared.

The group that was paid only $0.50 didn't have the luxury of looking to the payment to rationalize their behaviour. They still needed to resolve their dissonance and regain consistency in their lives. Without an adequate payment to help justify their essay, the only way was to change their attitude and express opinions that support what they were writing. They wrote essays that attacked their core beliefs, and yet they did it voluntarily. Why would they do this? In situations such as this, our self-talk tells us something is out of whack. How could any of us write an essay we don't believe a word of? The need to be consistent with the essay takes over. The essay writers questioned their original beliefs and found room for an alternative view. They considered how another perspective does have merit after all.

We all attempt to be consistent. This study shows how we can be influenced and persuaded to change our views and behaviour through very simple activities that appeal to our desire and need to avoid inconsistencies. Does this work in the real world or just with research studies?

Real-Life Dissonance

The practice of teaching and learning is a perfect example of consistency in real life. Students come to class with a world full of preconceived notions and attitudes that have been instilled in them since birth. Students walk into class with a desire to maintain these consistencies at all costs, and the teacher's job is to create new learning opportunities that will challenge these strongly held beliefs. How can teachers influence the students to be more receptive to new ideas and concepts? If these inconsistencies are large and the students are having difficulty solving their dissonance, then both the teacher and the student will have problems with the new material.

The same situation may apply to managing people. Let's say a manager wants to achieve certain behaviour in an employee but the employee is influenced by preconceived notions and disagrees with the approach. How does the manager achieve compliance in the face of this disagreement? The usual approach applied in business is to demand compliance using threats, which is the autocratic style. This rarely works long term. Preparing a strong argument and presenting the case forcefully may only reinforce the employee's previously held beliefs. If we push too hard and don't get the results we seek, we may end up making the problem far worse than it was in the first place. Sales is another excellent example. The pushy salesperson may lose the sale by being too forceful in challenging strongly held beliefs. It too may only serve to make those beliefs even stronger.

So what is the answer to overcoming someone's strongly held beliefs? The key is not to create dissonance forcefully, as the individual will simply justify their position even more so. An attack on people's beliefs rarely works. I suggest the art of self-discovery. This is what happened with the volunteers who wrote essays that were against their firmly held beliefs. They changed their attitudes because they volunteered. Self-discovery is an approach of asking yourself a variety of carefully crafted questions to help you draw fresh conclusions and slowly shift your attitudes. Self-discovery is an important component of both management and sales. Salespeople often do most of the talking, thinking they can convince clients to buy a product or service. Managers also do most of the talking, thinking they can convince employees to buy into change or corporate targets. The real challenge is to get employees to convince themselves to buy in.

The Foot-in-the-Door Technique

Gaining an early small commitment to something has been called the foot-in-the-door technique. Once the foot is in the door, people have accepted that you are there and will let the rest of you in. This age-old technique is based on very sound psychology.

Social scientists Jonathan Friedman and Scott Fraser published "Compliance without pressure: the foot-in-the-door technique" in the *Journal of Personality and Social Psychology* in 1966. In this study, they proved the power of starting with a little request before gaining a much larger request later. A researcher posed as a volunteer worker and went door to door in a residential neighbourhood in California, making a request that was ridiculous in nature and magnitude. Homeowners were asked to install a huge billboard on their front lawn in support of a public awareness initiative on driving safely in residential areas. The homeowner was even shown a photograph of a home with the huge sign already in place. The sign was so large that it virtually blocked the view of the house from the street and took up almost all of the front lawn. The sign simply read "Drive Carefully" in bold letters. In most instances, the homeowners turned down the request. Only 17 percent were willing to have the sign on their front lawn.

However, another group of residents in this same study agreed to have the sign erected on their front lawn a full 76 percent of the time. What was the difference? Why did this second group of homeowners agree so readily to the installation of such a huge and ugly sign on their lawn that basically disfigured their home? This segment of homeowners had been contacted two weeks earlier and had made a small commitment to the "Drive Carefully" campaign. A different researcher, again acting as a volunteer, had approached these homeowners, asking if they would put a small three-inch square sign in their window. The sign simply stated, "Be a Safe Driver." The request was so small and the cause a good one that most of the households canvassed agreed immediately to this small and inconsequential request. The homeowners dutifully installed the sign in their window and felt good about their contribution to the safety of their streets. Little did they know that this tiny commitment would lead to their agreement to a much larger request later.

These homeowners had made a commitment (and a public one at that) as supporters of safer streets. When a researcher returned two weeks later and made the larger request for the huge lawn sign, more than three quarters of those homeowners complied with the request. Once they had made a commitment to the small request, they needed to act consistent with the Drive Carefully philosophy and support the initiative with a huge lawn sign.

Those who made the small commitment first complied with the larger request almost four and a half times more often than those asked for the major commitment first. This increase in the rate of saying yes to a request was achieved by using the escalating commitment approach.

The researchers wanted to extend their research, so they approached a different set of homeowners and asked them if they would sign a petition to "keep California beautiful." Now who wouldn't sign a petition to keep their state or province beautiful? Almost everyone who was asked agreed immediately to the request and signed the petition. A new volunteer returned to these same homes two weeks later. This time they asked these residents to install the huge sign with the words "Drive Carefully" on their front lawns. The results are an amazing example of how we can influence our target audience with simple techniques. The people in this study agreed to the huge sign almost 50 percent of the time. These results are astounding. How could a commitment to a totally different subject influence the decision to accept a huge Drive Carefully sign on a lawn?

Even the researchers were baffled by these results. They pondered the question of why people would agree to the two disparate requests. They finally concluded that the simple act of signing the petition had changed the view the residents had of themselves.

Signing the petition led these homeowners to see themselves as activists who were interested in their community and had civic pride. They may never have considered themselves civic-minded individuals in the past, but the act of signing a petition had changed them. They needed to be consistent with their new commitment, and the only way to maintain harmony was to change their view to support their actions.

How To

We are susceptible to our desire to be consistent with our commitments and to be who we think we are. Successful managers realize that a small commitment can and often does lead to a much larger commitment later. These small commitments can change a person's self-image and make them willing to cooperate on issues they might not have otherwise.

In managing change, it might be wise to implement the changes in stages. Make very small changes first to gain commitments from employees. Once they help implement the changes, they will consider themselves change agents and will be much more willing to implement future changes. If you want your service people to call clients every day, you may want to start by having them call clients who have complemented the company or service. Once they see themselves as employees who communicate directly with clients, it's much easier to shift to changes that deal with customer complaints.

Bank tellers focus on reducing lineups, but management wants them to ask customers for more business—a huge shift in the way they see their job. Logic won't work, but a small specific step in the right direction will yield an attitude change that will change their behaviour, and they will *want* to do it. This is the key in any change management project. If a manager can get people to *want* to do something, the rest is easy.

When implementing change, break the change down to its simple components and ease your foot into the door. The components must be crystal clear to the employees effecting the change. Make them simple to accomplish and easy to understand, and you will move forward. Just because you pay employees doesn't always mean they will do what you want. If it were that easy, we wouldn't need managers.

Opposing Views

The challenge is that we simply don't want to hear any views that oppose our current outlook or worldview. Smokers, for example, know they should quit but refuse to read any anti-smoking magazine or news articles. They avoid dissonance by avoiding new information on the dangers of smoking and why they should quit. Do you know of managers who don't like bad news and will actually cut you off if you are about to share some reality with them? Managers who make a bad hiring decision will work twice as hard to help their new hire make the grade rather than admit they made an error.

The behaviour of stock investors reveals classic cases of justification. Investors will hang on to a stock whose value has recently declined and shows no prospect of recovering. The correct investment decision may be to take the loss and move on, but many somehow become attached to a loser stock because they hate to admit to a mistake. They need to act consistent with their initial decision to buy. I have often heard investors rationalize these decisions with, "It's not a loss until I sell it," or, "It's only a paper loss until the stock is actually sold." Sorry, folks, your net worth has declined, and I call that a loss.

In 1975, T. Moriarty published a study called "Crime, commitment, and the responsive bystander" in the *Journal of Personality and Social Psychology*. It's an interesting story demonstrating the power of influencing people to do something they wouldn't normally do. The study included staged thefts on a New York beach to see if onlookers would get involved and stop a crime in progress. The researchers set up an assistant on a beach towel with a radio.

The assistant would be a few feet away from someone lounging on the beach. After a few minutes of relaxing, the assistant would get up and walk away from the beach towel and radio and wander toward the water. Once they had left the scene, an accomplice would pose as a thief and steal the radio right in front of the subject. The pretend thief would grab the radio and run away in the classic grab-and-run style. This is New York, remember, so you can imagine that few people would react to this staged theft. In fact, hardly anyone was willing to put themselves at risk by attempting to stop the robbery. Not getting involved is a national pastime it would appear, as only four people out of the twenty attempts did anything to thwart the robbery.

The researchers also staged the theft with a slight adjustment to the circumstances. This change produced dramatically different results from the test subjects. The scenario was the same: An assistant relaxed on a beach towel with a radio close to the subject. This time, however, when the assistant got up to take a walk, they asked the adjacent subject for a favour: "Could you please watch my things?" Each time the assistant asked the question, he would wait for an affirmative answer. This ensured each subject had made a verbal commitment to a complete stranger. The results will astound you. The subjects attempted to stop the "thief" nineteen out of twenty times. They immediately responded by chasing him, grabbing the radio, and even physically restraining him, demanding an explanation.

The simple act of making a verbal commitment increased the desired response from 20 percent to a surprising 95 percent. Why would people, who normally don't want to get involved, respond so dramatically and aggressively to the theft of a radio? In the first instance, the subject made no commitment and was therefore not personally involved. They felt no personal obligation to stop the thief. The second set of subjects, on the other hand, made a verbal commitment to watch the radio and therefore had to act consistent with the promise when the radio was stolen. This was an immediate and automatic response to uphold their earlier commitment. The subjects were compelled to act consistent with their commitment even at personal risk. This is indeed a powerful influence tool.

Walk the Talk

Managers and other executives need to show behaviour consistent with the words they use to communicate with employees. Many managers, however, don't "walk the talk"; they just talk, and employees notice the disparity between words and actions. In this case, actions speak louder than words, and the inconsistent manager is seen as untrustworthy, indecisive, or, even worse, an out-and-out liar. People don't like to follow a leader whose words are inconsistent with actions. It disrupts harmony at the office, and employees have difficulty performing at their peak. Chit-chat and gossip often takes over the workplace as well. Employees will try to deal with the inconsistency by lowering their assessment of company leadership and the company itself.

The Up-Sell Technique

By the same token, if you can get someone to commit to a product, an idea, or a decision, that person is more likely to remain committed even after the terms and conditions of the original situation change.

New car dealers use this tactic effectively. Once you have decided on our beautiful new car, you become committed to owning that vehicle. You love the colour, you love the smell, and you love the way you feel when you sit inside it. This is when consistency moves in. Now that you have decided you want the car, you will respond favourably to the undercoating to keep the car like new longer. You may even go for the permanent wax job to keep that showroom shine for five years. The process of buying a car is all about getting a commitment. The dealer lets you take it for a ride, and some even let you take the car home. When you wow the neighbours, you become committed. The paperwork seems endless, all part of enhancing the commitment. Sometimes even the price of the car was low at the beginning only to rise after the dealer sees the commitment signals on your face.

Will You?

In the restaurant business, no-shows are a real problem. People phone up a restaurant to make a reservation for dinner and then don't show up. The restaurant holds the table and perhaps turns away other paying guests while under the assumption that the people who made the reservation will arrive and take the table. This has been a serious issue for restaurant owners for many years. Some restaurants have solved the problem by not allowing reservations at all and simply operating on a first-come, first-served basis. This works, but not for everyone. Many people still want to make a reservation so they can be assured of a table at a particular time to avoid a long wait.

Some restaurants have attempted to solve the no-show problem by asking for a credit card and charging a fee if you don't show or cancel the same day. This didn't work too well because people simply didn't make reservations any longer or decided to go elsewhere. Hotels have implemented the practice of taking a credit card to hold the room and will charge you if you cancel with less than twenty-four hours' notice. Hotels seemed to have been able to implement this without undue difficulty. Perhaps reserving a room is more important than reserving a restaurant table.

Restaurants that I have dealt with are quite polite and will usually say something like, "Please call if you have to cancel your reservation." I recently noticed several restaurants have changed this common statement to something different. On further investigation, I discovered that this new approach has reduced no-shows significantly. They added two words to the statement provided by their hostess. Think about it for a minute. What two words could a restaurant add to this previous statement to get people to call if they want to cancel their reservation? Think of this in terms of commitment and consistency. What could the hostess say to get a commitment from people to call to cancel their reservation?

The two words were *will you*, and they immediately helped decrease no-shows at these two restaurants significantly. What is the difference here? The first is a statement: "Please call if you have to cancel your reservation." The second is a question: "Will you please call if you have to cancel your reservation?" In the first instance, the person on the phone didn't have to answer. They could mumble something and not make a commitment. They therefore felt no internal pressure to call to cancel. When you turn the statement into a question, the person must answer, and the answer will always be, "Yes. I will call."

A simple change of forcing the client to make a verbal commitment increases the probability that they will act consistent and follow through on their promise. The key here is to pause after the question and give the client a chance to respond. When they do, a little switch flips inside the brain. We all want to be true to our word. Our word is our bond, after all. We are not born liars; we want to keep our promises and will act diligently to keep them. The challenge, of course, is to get a commitment first. In this instance, it was quite easy, and the results proved to be dramatic. It worked much in the same way as the story in the chapter on reciprocity about the mother with her stubborn son who didn't want to put on his snowsuit.

Most managers seem to prefer making a statement when requesting rather than actually asking a question and getting a commitment. It's a simple shift in approach, but the results can be astounding.

Effort Extra

Another interesting aspect of human nature is what I call the big-effort syndrome. It would appear that the more energy, time, or money we put into a commitment, the more we want to stick with it. We see this in business all the time. Executives get tied to a bad idea because they had made a public commitment to it and allocated significant resources to a project. They would sooner throw good money after bad than admit the idea was wrong. Cutting your losses is extremely difficult if the commitment has involved significant resources both personal and financial.

When a manager hires someone, there is a lot riding on ensuring the new employee is successful. The higher the level of management that chooses the new employee, the greater the degree of commitment to ensuring this person works out. People are quite hesitant to fire an employee they have hired personally. These new hires will experience more chances to fail and will receive more encouragement to succeed than those who have been hired by someone else. The public commitment displayed by the hiring will force the manager to try to justify the decision and find ways to keep an incompetent or incompatible employee on staff long after they should.

The New Hire

A number of years ago, my vice president hired a new assistant vice president, George (not his real name). The new hire to the company had wonderful credentials, a good resume, and experience, and he was a friend of the VP—not a close friend, but a friend just the same. George was well aware of this relationship and therefore felt more secure in the role than he might otherwise have been.

It didn't take long for the people reporting to George to realize that the cultural fit was terribly wrong. The company had been an entrepreneurial one and encouraged employees to be independent and empowered to do the right things for the customer. The staff had previously been encouraged to share customer issues up the ladder as a way to resolve them quickly. George, on the other hand, had an autocratic approach, and he wanted to ensure that his people made him look good. He told the staff to follow the chain of command or face termination. He told them not to bring up customer concerns, as it would make him look bad.

The team reporting directly to George started to go underground rather than be open and honest. They talked among themselves and complained constantly. Many started to look for work elsewhere. Human resources told the VP about the management problems the team was facing. The VP claimed it was just a change in management and that all would be fine shortly. He said he would coach George and bring him around. Well, as you can expect, things went from bad to worse, and the VP felt that some of the employees were wrongfully accusing George of things. The VP even wanted to terminate several of George's people. The justification game was in full swing. He had to find the source of performance problems within the staff to justify that his hire had been the correct decision. This went on for a year with ever-escalating issues exacerbated by George's lack of management skills. The autocratic approach became more pronounced as George started to see he was getting into trouble. He blamed others in the company for his problems, and the VP actually believed the problem lied elsewhere in the organization. Interviews with some disgruntled staff merely led to more coaching but no tangible results. George simply was not a cultural fit for the organization, and after a year, the VP finally had to admit he made an error and terminated George.

Why did it take so long for an intelligent and effective VP to make a decision to terminate a problem manager? The staff constantly wondered why the VP couldn't see the damage George was causing to the culture and the morale of the team. They started to lose confidence in the VP after six months of inaction and soon started to lose confidence in the company. This is a severe consequence of not dealing with an ugly situation early.

George lasted as long as he did because of the simple fact that the VP had made a public commitment and needed to act consistently. The extra effort involved in hiring a new executive influenced the VP's ability to make the right decision. In feeling compelled to justify his hiring decision, he deferred his firing decision. The VP felt his judgement would be in question if he fired

George too soon, but by waiting too long, his judgement and integrity was in question anyway. It's a catch-22 really. Too soon hurts the VP's self-image, and waiting too long hurts the company's image of the VP. A good rule of thumb might be to do the right thing based on facts rather than the effort put into the situation. If we are aware of the influence that our drive for consistency can have on us, we will be empowered to deal with problems more effectively and make the right decisions quickly.

Managing Commitments

Since we all have a personal requirement to be consistent, a manager's job then becomes to gain initial commitments when tackling an issue or instituting a change. Those who make commitments will be more willing to agree to further requests that are in line with the initial position they take. These smaller commitments are most effective when they are public, require some effort, and come from within rather than forced by another. These commitments are powerful and have a tendency to be supported long after their usefulness has expired, even when they are misguided.

To gain a commitment, we actually have to ask for it. Many managers are reluctant to ask in fear of employees disagreeing or refusing. This is why we start small with the goal of getting a yes. When asking for a commitment, we should pause, look the person in the eye, and wait for a response. Once the yes comes, a commitment is made.

Written commitments are even better than verbal commitments. The coaching process we will discuss uses written and verbal commitments regularly. These help employees commit to forming new behaviours that will move them forward. As managers, we can and should use the psychology of human nature to improve performance.

Best Practices

1. Be very specific when outlining small changes.

2. Clarify exactly what people need to do and ask for commitments.

3. Ask for small commitments first.

4. Use questions rather than statements and commands—use "will you" when making requests.

5. Wait for people to say yes before moving on—people want to keep their promises.

6. Keep your promises as manager—match your words with your actions.

7. Empower your people by letting them make decisions.

Chapter 9
Authority

Managers often use their authority to get things done simply because they can. They also have a regrettable tendency to be unduly influenced by authority. An authority figure such as a doctor or manager will often have credibility and influence simply by virtue of their title. We seem to set aside our normal rational thought processes and blindly believe someone in authority, and we will often do as they request without question in many instances. We assume these authority figures have more knowledge or more expertise in certain areas. We have a tendency to trust them. Many authority figures such as doctors do in fact have a high level of expertise, and it makes perfectly good sense to trust them and do as they recommend.

Authority can be a powerful tool of influence in management as long as it's not abused. Too many managers simply use their title as their authority while really not having developed true authority. There are various ways to enhance authority and credibility. The most effective authority figure is credible, both in terms of knowledge and trustworthiness.

Here is a simple management-related question that many face when dealing with a presentation to staff. You have a weakness in your change proposal, as most change initiatives have. When should you mention this weakness? The choices are: 1) early in the conversation, 2) in the middle of the conversation, 3) at the end of the conversation, or 4) not during the conversation at all. Now remember that most products or services have some type of weakness associated with them; however, for this question, let's assume that it's a small weakness.

The Question

You have a weakness in your recommendation and have to decide when to mention it (if at all). Now write your answer based on the above-mentioned choices so you can refer back to it.

I have asked this question of over 3,000 salespeople in my research, and the answers always indicate a great variety of responses. I will usually present to groups of salespeople in the same role in the same company, and I am surprised at the disagreement that occurs when we discuss the answers. It seems there is no specific training around this question of when to present a weakness. Many suggest mentioning it in the middle, which is called the toasted sandwich technique: You slide the weakness in between the cheese and the lettuce and hope the client won't notice the weakness at all. It gets sandwiched between the features and the benefits. Others suggest mentioning it at the end because if you lay out a successful sales pitch, the client is already sold and the weakness given at the end will be an afterthought with little impact on the outcome. This is called the carpet sales technique: When you're finished the sale, you reach down and pull the carpet out from under the client. If the client is still standing, you have a sale.

Some have suggested they would never mention a weakness unless the customer asks about it, as it may not be a weakness at all. There's no sense in raising an issue that may not even be an issue. Finally, some say to mention the weakness at the beginning just to get it out of the way so they can overcome the weakness with additional features and benefits. It also seems that many salespeople think the client will forget about the weakness as they proceed with the features and benefits. These salespeople must believe clients have short-term memory problems.

The Answer

What is the correct answer? Most people I have interviewed focus on the product rather than look at what the customer really wants from a salesperson. I always suggest that the customer really wants to buy from someone who is knowledgeable and trustworthy. Salespeople often forget that what they are really selling is themselves. The client wants affirmation early in the conversation that they can trust the salesperson.

Outlining a weakness early in the conversation clearly tells the client that you are both knowledgeable about the product's features and benefits and honest enough to explain the pros and the cons. This may lead the client to think, "Wow! This person really knows their stuff, and they are even honest enough to showcase the pros and cons to really give me a clear picture of what I'm buying." This communicates to the client that you are an authority on the subject and honest enough to give the straight goods.

Whatever you say after this impression of knowledge and honesty will be ingrained in your client's mind—it will have much more impact. The client will be much more willing to buy from you. People want to buy from people they trust. Would you buy a house from someone you didn't trust? Would you invest your retirement funds with an advisor you didn't trust? None of us would. We all want to deal with people we trust. This simple strategy will enhance a feeling of trust between you and your client. The client will have a more positive relationship with you, as they will trust what you will say next. This is when to outline the features and benefits—when they will have much more impact on the client.

The same logic applies to you as a manager. To get eager compliance from employees, a manager must be seen as honest and knowledgeable. This will increase your level of authority, and your team's respect for you will skyrocket. They will be much more likely to want to say yes to your ideas—they will, in fact, be eager to.

Weakness First

Marketing companies use the weakness-first strategy quite effectively. For example, "Listerine: the taste you hate three times a day." Buckley's, however, is the classic case of using it to persuade you that their product works. They are quite upfront in telling consumers that their product tastes terrible but works. What would happen if they didn't tell you about the taste in the marketing ads? You buy the product, take it home, pour some of the liquid onto a spoon, and take a sip. "*Wow!*" would be your immediate reaction. "This stuff tastes terrible." The next thing you'd do is check the expiry date to see if the product has gone bad, because no product should taste like this. Even if you discover that the date is fine, you might assume the product must have gone bad and throw out the entire bottle. This would be a case of the product's taste being the weakness, and the company didn't inform the customer.

In reality, Buckley's openly advertises that the product tastes terrible. So when we buy some and take a spoonful, we expect it to taste terrible. And they're right, we think, it's horrible, therefore it must work. The fact that Buckley's tells you it tastes bad creates a sense of credibility in the company, which in turn tells us that their promise of their product working must also be true. It's an incredibly effective marketing strategy that works again and again on all of us, and Buckley's has created a huge brand around their product's bad taste. This is a classic example of using a product weakness upfront to build trust and persuade people to buy it anyway.

On the Job

As a manager, you need to implement some new service standards for your team. What is the weakness that the team will perceive? It's usually well known before the meeting, and you should expect it to come up as an objection. If you expect an objection, you should raise the objection yourself. This demonstrates the weakness-first strategy and will help enhance your knowledge and credibility so that the rest of your presentation will ring true and be much more readily accepted as fair and equitable. If you let someone else raise the objection, you will appear defensive (or may actually be defensive), and the employee will want to argue to protect their objection—a lose/lose situation.

I know this approach seems unusual, but we all know every plan has a few weaknesses in it. It's the final execution, however, that really makes the difference, and this is where the employees come in. They must execute plans with a passion to make them work. Being open and honest enhances your authority and increases the respect your employees have for you. It will be much easier to gain commitments to any new initiative if you are honest upfront.

If you demand compliance and install detailed follow-up mechanisms to ensure compliance, you are running an autocratic system, and you will never get maximum performance in this kind of environment. Every manager should reassess the way they communicate and shift from demanding people to act to influencing people to act.

Authority

Authority is essentially the power to influence thought, opinion, or behaviour. It has an amazing power over all of us, and it influences our daily lives. Authority has been the subject of research in a variety of settings from the family (parental authority); small groups or teams (informal authority of leadership); organizations such as churches, schools, business, and bureaucracies; and even nations.

Most religions around the world consider God as the supreme authority. God is believed to have the ultimate authority and wisdom, which far exceeds that of mere mortals. This divine being provides rules, regulations, and directions for all of us to follow. This authority is unquestioned by the devout. Faith in the divine wisdom of God overrules individual decision-making and provides guidelines for behaviour. The Ten Commandments clearly demonstrate the word of God and carry tremendous authority with the faithful.

Religions have used this authority of divine beings to influence behaviour for millennia. Authority is a powerful tool for all of us to consider when we want to be more influential.

What are some of the aspects of authority that provide the power to influence? The classic example of parental authority in action is the phrase "Because I said so." Children are always asking questions and questioning decisions. They use the word *why* thousands of times during their childhood, and as they get older, they shift to *why not*. Rather than explain things logically to children, we as parents often fall back on the authority principle and respond with, "Because I said so." Most of us actually believe this strategy will work. This parental authority is a timesaving tool for parents. "Because I said so" doesn't make the assertion true or false, but it certainly clarifies who has the authority in the relationship. There is no need for additional proof in this instance, as the simple statement holds credibility because of the authority held by parents. We expect obedience with this simple phrase. We don't always get it, however, and that is the beauty and challenge of parenting.

The word *because* seems to have a power of its own to convince people to say yes. My son was in the Gap recently to buy a sweater. He said to the clerk, "Will you give me a discount on this sweater because its sunny outside?" The clerk looked at him and agreed to give a 10 percent discount. When we hear "because," it sends an automatic signal to our brain that there must be a good reason for the request, and we feel obliged to say yes. Managers, take heed of this simple approach. When making a request, say "because" when you provide the why.

In the business world, we all want to be more influential. We want to convince others that our ideas are the best ones. We want to move people to our way of thinking. We want to influence a client to buy from us, or we want employees to do what we want them to do. We even want to influence our friends in social settings.

I had a manager once who always used the VP's name in discussions. He would say, "I was talking to John, and he feels we should implement a specific plan." Rather than use his own authority or persuasive techniques, he relied on the authority of a more senior person to support his initiatives. This is tougher to deal with, but after a few times, it's easy to spot. Quite often the story is just that—a story. Maybe this manager had never even mentioned his project to his boss but invoked the authority of the big boss anyway. If you use this technique, do yourself a favour and manage directly instead. Your people want to deal with you.

These people simply opt out of leading by themselves and require coaching to take more responsibility for decisions. Managers have shifted responsibility upwards in organizations since the beginning of management. This is similar to the parental refrain "Wait until your father gets home." Rather than deal with issues, they delegate them to another who seems to have more authority and are therefore more likely to get the task accomplished. I suggest instead that we all take responsibility for what is in front of us. We all have the power to be in charge of our lives.

We don't have to exercise our authority blatantly just because we are a manager. Great managers influence and persuade; they don't demand. It's interesting to note that many autocratic managers don't really have the authority to make lasting changes. They're excellent at making short-term changes but cannot effect behavioural change that improves performance and results without constantly having to follow-up and give directions.

When managers use legitimate authority and earn the respect of their teams, people want to do what's right. There is a big difference in performance when people *have* to so something versus when they *want* to do something.

Clothing

Clothing is another influential tool that stimulates an automatic response of compliance. Leonard Bickman published a research study in the *Journal of Applied Social Psychology* entitled "The social power of a uniform." In the study, they arranged for a researcher dressed in normal street clothes to ask pedestrians to pick up a piece of litter or to stand on the other side of a bus stop sign. They documented the number of times the pedestrians complied with the request. They then changed the attire of the researcher and had him wear a security guard uniform. The researcher in the uniform made the same request to the pedestrians, and the results were documented. The results clearly indicated that people obeyed the request from a researcher in the uniform far more often than they did when dressed in street clothes.

In a similar study, the pedestrians were told, "See that guy over there by the meter? He is overparked but doesn't have any change. Give him a dime!" The researcher then stepped around the corner so he would be out of sight when the subject reached the man by the parked car. Nearly all of the pedestrians complied with the request to give the man a dime when requested by the researcher in a security guard uniform, but only half did so when requested by an individual in normal street clothes. This occurred even though the requester was no longer visible. The power of the uniform influenced subjects to comply even when physically absent.

As a manager, it's important to be good but also to look good. If you need to be more persuasive in certain situations and need support from your team, then dress with a little authority and you will gain agreement much easier. People who wear black or navy blue suits are believed more often than those in any other colour. So if you have a major meeting with executives or with your team, wear black or blue. If you're nervous, wear your favourite outfit. You know you look good in this one. If you want to appear friendly and approachable, wear soft pastel colours. It seems weird, but the psychology is there to back you up, and it works.

Gestures

As a manager, gestures are an important aspect of your ability to communicate to your team. Eye contact has always been used as a method to demonstrate authority. If someone looks us in the eye, we assume they are telling the truth. Liars are believed to look away when the actual lie is being delivered.

Hand gestures and body language convey tremendous information to audiences, who also convey information back to speakers. A gesture of open hands usually means an openness and honesty. Rejection is inferred when arms are crossed, and it usually means a tough sell is ahead. If the hands move to the hip, we are in real trouble, as this is a defiant move. Shaking of the leg or wetting the lips is usually a sign of stress, and a good manager should look to relieve stress. Lying has many clues, such as touching the face or mouth, downcast eyes especially to the left, shifting in a seat, or rubbing sweaty hands on a pant leg. Excessive scratching of the nose or pulling at the ear is another telltale sign that a fib is on the way.

There are a number of books on this subject that would make good reading if this topic interests you. I have only scratched the surface of non-verbal communication. The key to presenting or talking to people is to be aware of the non-verbal cues that will influence your message's credibility. This will help guide you in your communication.

The Voice

The voice is also a powerful tool. Remember George H. W. Bush when he was president of the United States? The weekly comedy show *Saturday Night Live* had a field day with his voice. Comedian Dana Carvey boosted his career with his recurring imitation of Bush's hesitant style. Bush lost the next election to a man with a more powerful presence: Bill Clinton, a master communicator.

As a manager, communication is your most important tool, and yet very few pay any attention to the way we communicate. Decisive and fast talkers are really no surer of their facts than anyone else, but their style creates the impression of confidence in what they have to say. Audiences sense this confidence, and they in turn assume the speaker has more credibility. The good communicator is seen as more intelligent, knowledgeable, and authoritative on the topic presented. This is the reason why many professional sales-people or those in management join Toastmasters clubs or take courses in public speaking. An enhanced delivery style is another influential tool.

Even the volume of the voice is important. Louder voices are considered to be more authoritative, and the words being delivered also seem to carry more credibility. When parents raise their voices, children all of sudden know that they mean business and will usu-ally comply with the request quickly. If, of course, the raised voice is a normal occurrence, it does lose its impact, as many of us know. Judicial use of an elevated voice enhances the authority of a speaker and increases the level of influence.

The next time you're watching television, notice the change in volume for commercials. The volume of commercials is elevated well above the volume for the show you're watching. This tech-nique is believed to add credibility to the information provided in the commercial. There is a reason for everything, and it usually has to do with influencing people.

Authority in Management

In the right hands, authority is a powerful tool for motivating peo-ple. We all listen more attentively to an authority figure, and we have a natural tendency to trust those with authority. Your employ-ees will more readily follow you if they perceive you as an author-ity figure in their lives. The title does give you an edge, but not for long. You need to back it up with your performance.

The guidelines outlined above will help you position yourself as the authority figure in your department or branch. The rest is up to you. Raise your profile in the company by becoming more ef-fective, or let it diminish. Don't forget that those who are perceived as an authority figure are also more likely to be promoted.

Best Practices

1. People will say yes more often to those they perceive as authoritative.

2. The most effective authority is credible authority with both knowledge and honesty.

3. Present a weakness early in your presentation to gain credibility.

4. People believe in people they trust—gain their trust early.

5. Be persuasive, not demanding.

6. Dress and act the part.

7. Speak loudly, with clear enunciation, and with purpose.

8. Showcase your industry credentials for all to see.

Chapter 10
I Like You, You Like Me

All things being equal in the value proposition between competing products or services, people will always choose to buy from people they like. It's interesting to note that even when all things are unequal in the value proposition, people will generally still choose to buy from people they like. This is certainly not new to the experienced salesperson, but it may be to the experienced manager.

The liking principle is another powerful tool that can influence and persuade others to move in our chosen direction. We will look into the various aspects of why people like others and what activities we can engage in to get people to like us quickly. People will follow people they like, people trust people they like, and people will change their behaviour for people they like.

Who Do You Like?
Who do you like better Oprah Winfrey or Donald Trump? Both are celebrities, both are extremely influential, both are wealthy, and both have qualities we admire. I think it's fair to say that most people would say they like Oprah better. Why is it that most would say they like Oprah better than Donald Trump? What impact does this likeability factor have on Oprah's ability to influence the average person? If Oprah puts her seal of approval on a book, it's virtually guaranteed to be a best seller. We like Oprah and trust her, so when she makes a recommendation, we believe her and believe the book is worth purchasing and reading. That is influence of a high level

from someone we have never even met.

Why would so many people be influenced by what Oprah Winfrey likes and dislikes? The true test of her influence can be assessed in the 2008 United States presidential election. For the first time in her career, Oprah Winfrey decided to openly support a presidential candidate. She was on the hustings with presidential candidate Senator Barack Obama.

Donald Trump, on the other hand, is not as likeable because he appears too opinionated perhaps, and we believe he may have ulterior motives in his recommendations. He remains interesting and we love to hear The Donald rant about issues; however, he may be perceived as self-serving while Oprah is seen as community serving.

Former American president Bill Clinton may be the classic case of one who demonstrates the principle of liking overpowering facts. It allowed Clinton to remain in the presidency and continue to be influential even during impeachment proceedings. If Bill Clinton were able to run for president again, I believe he would win based on the fact that people simply like him. Why would so many set aside his wrongdoings, big and small, and continue to like him? What is it about Clinton that just seems to draw people to him?

The Likeability Factor

Likeability may be one of the most influential tools we have, and yet we rarely use it to our advantage to help build relationships. Have a look at your friends. Why are they friends? You will find that they share similarities with you. You have common interests. There is a sense of cooperation between friends. We like people who work with us cooperatively. Finally, we like people who like us and tell us.

People are more persuaded by those they like. Why are we influenced this way? Why wouldn't we simply rely on the facts of the situations rather than be influenced by those who have managed to make us like them? It all goes back to the statement about honesty. People trust those who they perceive as honest and believe what they say. People we like are perceived as being more honest and trustworthy than those we don't know and certainly more than those we don't like. It's human nature. Marketing companies, salespeople, managers, and virtually everyone who wishes to influence our behaviour tap into this as this tactic, and we are exposed to it on a daily basis.

Home Sales Parties

The Tupperware party is a great example of many of the influence principles outlined in this book. Many companies have now implemented the home party approach where hosts invite friends to their home to showcase the products. Theses parties range from kitchenware all the way to sex toys and lingerie, but the basic premise is always the same.

The host earns a sales commission. Sometimes the salesperson is the actual host, but often a professional presenter arrives to showcase the wares. Either way, the same persuasive techniques are at play. The real power in these transactions comes from the host. All the guests know the host, and the party is at the host's home. The guests are influenced to think they are buying from a friend and feel an obligation to actually purchase something after being invited into their home. If you have never been to one of these parties, I suggest you attend one and witness the techniques involved and observe how you feel as requests for sales are made. I guarantee you will feel a strong obligation to make a purchase.

Consumer researchers have investigated the impact of these home sales parties and have confirmed the effectiveness of this approach. The social bond created by inviting friends is twice as likely to determine product sales than the features and benefits of the product itself. People are more influenced by friendship and liking the host than by the product. These companies know this, and it's interesting to note that the guests know this as well. My wife has decided that she won't attend any more of these parties, as she invariably buys something she doesn't need because of the obligation to buy something. But when a friend calls to invite her to a party, she struggles with the obligation to attend. She is torn between wanting to attend to please her friend and the desire not to attend, as she knows she will come home with something new. Pleasing the friend usually wins the day, and we have Christmas gifts for our children for the next three years.

These companies know all about the psychology of liking and influence, and it's a market worth billions.

Managing Likeability

How can managers use the likeability factor to get teams to perform well? The first step is to get support from individuals on the team before initiating a change. If some of the more respectful team members are in favour of the change, then others will also feel obliged to support it. It's important, however, to be careful not to use this tool in a manipulative way because it can backfire if it's not all legitimate. You basically bring in some team members to discuss the new change and get their commitment before communicating it to the rest of the team. This small group may in fact even be able to provide suggestions and enhancements, so it's a good idea for a few reasons.

Getting support from team members whom the rest of the group trusts is an effective way to get things done quickly with minimum disruption. It sure beats being autocratic and demanding that everyone comply or else.

First Impressions

Let's take a closer look at some of the factors that influence our propensity to like someone immediately. This is when we make a great first impression or perform well during what we call "the moment of truth." First impressions do have an enormous influence over our perceptions. When we meet someone for the very first time, we all have a tendency to draw a conclusion about that person immediately and then spend the rest of the conversation looking for things that reinforce our opinion of them. It's a natural occurrence that's almost impossible to curtail. This is why first impressions are a critical element in whether we will get a person to like us. It also means it's a critical element in our ability to influence that person.

It's not just our first impressions on people either; it's first impressions on every aspect of life that comes into play. You walk into a restroom in a restaurant, and it's dirty. Where does your mind go next? If they can't keep the bathroom clean, what does the kitchen look like? Now the food will taste a little off—that is, if you even decide to stay.

One time I was flying back from a presentation I had made in Arizona. When I got to my seat, I noticed a napkin stuck in the little pouch on the back of the seat in front of me. Being curious, I reached in and pulled out the napkin. Well, much to my surprise, I discovered a small piece of pizza. What do you think happened next in my impressionable mind? I thought, "Well, if the airline can't even clean the inside of the plane, I wonder what the engine maintenance is like. Are the pilots experienced? Do they have enough fuel for the trip?"

Just as these thoughts were going through my mind, I heard a different noise coming out of the engine as the plane started to move. I looked out my window at the wing and engine and noticed that several of the bolts looked loose. I poked the passenger beside me and said, "Did you hear that noise? It seemed unusual to me."

He just looked over and said, "No. That's normal."

I looked out the window again, and the noise seemed even louder. As I stared at the engine, I noticed that several bolts holding the engine on the wing seemed to be moving. I poked the guy beside me again and said, "Look out the window. Those bolts on the engine look loose."

He simply said, "Look, everything is fine, there is nothing wrong with this plane, and don't poke me anymore."

I was in a state of panic. I don't like to fly all that much in the first place, and now the engine was making strange noises, bolts were loose, and the wing even seemed to wobble.

The entire flight was horrible for me. I kept hearing unusual noises. Every time the seatbelt sign came on, I knew we were out of fuel and going down in a farmer's field somewhere. Even the seats felt lumpy. All this happened because my first impression was influenced by a napkin with a piece of pizza in it. I was looking for ways to justify my first impression that the airline was sloppy, and I was creative in what I used to justify it. My first impression was that this airline was careless in the little things and therefore they must be careless about the really important things too. It wasn't until the plane touched down on the airfield that I felt better. A bad flight made much worse because of a piece of leftover pizza. First impressions count.

As a manager, first impressions of you occur every day you go to work and every time to you talk to an employee. Your employees are watching you carefully to ascertain clues about how to behave and what's important. We all send signals to be interpreted, so as a manager, you should be aware of what this moment can do to the perception of your plans, your ideas, or your proposed changes.

Appearance—Do You Look Good?

Does a person's appearance influence the moment of truth? It's generally acknowledged that attractive people have an advantage in a social setting. It's also recognized that this advantage goes far beyond mere social settings. We immediately draw conclusions about people based simply on their appearance. These conclusions occur immediately and influence our perceptions of people. Generally speaking, attractive people are immediately assigned positive qualities such as honesty, intelligence, kindness, and talent. We immediately like these people and have a desire to be around them. We believe they have more fun, have more money, and have more exciting careers. Most of us would deny that we make this automatic judgement but may believe others might. Attractive people do tend to have an advantage in life, and we give it to them unknowingly.

It seems we try to please people we like and find attractive.

Do blondes really have more fun? Alan S. Miller and Satoshi Kanazawa's article entitled "Ten Politically Incorrect Truths About Human Nature" published in *Psychology Today* magazine points out that long before blondes were immortalized in movies, women were dying their hair blonde. As early as the fifteenth century, women were dying their hair blonde to be more appealing, and apparently it worked. Blonde hair evokes a sense of youth and vigour, and it appears more attractive. Many of us immediately like someone with blonde hair. Certainly, the number of blondes suggests this preference, as many of the blondes are not blonde at all. We as observers know this, but it doesn't change our immediate reaction to blonde hair. Check this out yourself. The next time you see two women walking away from you, one a blonde and the other a brunette, notice which one your eyes linger on a little longer. Even though we will consciously refute any preference for blondes or for attractive people in general, there is much happening on a subconscious level.

The judicial system may be an even better example, as its outcomes are supposed to be based on the decisions of an unbiased jury after reviewing the evidence of each case. In the study "Is justice really blind? The effect of litigant physical attractiveness on judicial judgment" published in the *Journal of Applied Social Psychology*, researchers rated the attractiveness of seventy-four male defendants at the start of their criminal trials. The researchers later reviewed the court records for the decisions in these cases. They found that the handsome men received significantly lighter sentences and were twice as likely to avoid jail time all together. The same study also revealed that fines were twice as high when the victim was better looking than the defendant.

The Halo Effect

The aspect of psychology based on appearance has been called the halo effect. Basically, it occurs when one positive attribute affects other people's perceptions of an individual. The good quality becomes so powerful that it overcomes all other attributes, and the perception of that individual becomes much more positive. Many HR professionals know how this works when managers provide performance reviews. If the manager likes the employee, the review is always more positive than if the manager feels neutral. An attractive person through the halo effect becomes smarter, more effective, and more knowledgeable. As we've seen with the judicial system, the halo effect results in lighter fines and sentences.

As most HR professionals and managers already know, attractive people get jobs quicker and get better jobs. The results of a study on grooming in hiring situations were outlined in the article "Female applicants' grooming and personnel selection" published in the *Journal of Social Behavior and Personality*. In a simulated interview, the candidates with good grooming accounted for more favourable hiring decisions than did actual job qualifications. The interviewers even claimed that appearance played a very small role in their decision-making process.

Now it becomes clear why attractive women are in car ads and why trade shows always have attractive people at their booths. It would appear that attractive women can persuade men more easily than unattractive women, and by the same token, it would appear that attractive men can persuade women more easily than unattractive men. The halo effect comes into play. We automatically attribute unassociated skills and traits to attractive people, and yes, we automatically like them better too. If we like them better, we are more susceptible to their influence as well. As a manager, if you remain aware of the halo effect, perhaps you will learn to be more balanced in hiring decisions and assessing performance and not be so swayed by your personal likes. It's tough to do, but if you simply become aware of it, you are halfway home.

You can also use the halo effect to your own advantage. If you improve your appearance, you will be liked quickly and will enhance your ability to influence and persuade those around you. The objective is to make a positive first impression and enhance the opportunity to be liked immediately. The objective is to have your clients or your team reinforce your strengths rather than look for those weaknesses we all have. We have both strengths and weakness, so the challenge is to showcase our strengths in that all-important first twenty seconds of meeting a client or a new team member. Here are some suggestions to think about when preparing to meet people for the first or second time:

1. Comb that hair, dress up rather than down, and put on a little makeup to enhance your natural beauty. You only get a single opportunity to make a good first impression, and it happens every day as a manager. Look professional, and you will be perceived as professional and be more influential.

2. Each of us is equipped with one of the most influential tools available. This tool significantly enhances first impressions immediately. It's your teeth. That's right. A smile is the first thing people will notice when they see you. Think of going into a bank, a car dealership, or to the checkout at the grocery store, and the people there have no teeth visible. What's your impression of them? What are your impressions of that store, of the management of the people, and even of the products they sell? Take a moment right now and look in a mirror. Close your mouth without a hint of a smile. Take a good look. Now smile and show some of those lovely teeth. What a difference. People who smile automatically appear more receptive, they are seen as open and welcoming and even more trustworthy. As a manager wanting to be more influential, your simple ability to smile is an invaluable tool. Be observant in the marketplace and in

social settings. The people who smile tend to have more people around them.

3. Consider implementing these tips around the greeting aspect of any interaction, be it business, social, or personal. Before meeting clients, look in the mirror, check your hair and clothes, and smile a big smile with lots of teeth. This does two things. First, it allows you to check your teeth for any food that might have been lodged there at lunchtime. Second, it shows you how good a smile can be. You will notice that you feel better instantly.

4. People's names are very important to them. Many companies implement name tags for employees, which is really designed to allow managers and executives to know and use the person's name. We are all drawn to people who know our name, and we immediately like them better. When everyone knows everyone else by name, teams and employees naturally work better together.

Similarity

People like people who are similar to them. Look at your friends. Sure enough, one of the reasons you like these friends is because they are similar to you in some way. It may be a similarity of opinions, personality traits, background, culture, hobbies, or even proximity.

Many studies have shown that we have a tendency to like people who are like us. This allows us to relate to them in a more positive way. People-watching is a marvellous pastime many of us engage in, and it's interesting to note that people at a party or business function will gravitate towards people who seem to be similar to them in some way. Men in business suits will be gathered together while those in business casual will be ensconced in another corner. The artistic types will be gathered in another corner. I attend a lot of business functions that are basically social events for networking, and circulating is part of the job of a networker. It's interesting to note that conversations are short and superficial until you find someone with a common interest. Suddenly, you like that individual immediately. It may be a common interest in fishing, golf, job specialty, or culture. The words flow much easier now, as a bond has been created simply through the act of finding a similarity.

We seem to like and trust people who are similar to us in some fashion. There are now experts at selecting jurors for trials, and part of their agenda is to choose jurors who have a similarity to the accused. If jurors feel they share some commonality with the accused, they will be more likely to associate with that individual and even begin to like them for these similarities. This is rooted in our subconscious, of course, but this mode of jury selection is a powerful strategy in giving the accused a much better chance of being acquitted or at least receiving a reduced sentence.

A manager can develop stronger team ties by encouraging employees to find similarities among each other to create bonds. When people like each other at work, they work better together; they are more creative and more efficient. Employees will also be less territorial about their workplace when trust grows among them. This may seem a simple thing, but this is a unique way for managers to develop teamwork. Below are some tips to help create bonds through similarities:

1. Take the time to find similarities between you and your people individually. Be a person as well as a manager. During your one-on-one discussions, ask your employees opened-ended questions to learn as much as you can about them so you can find similarities with them. This will significantly enhance your relationships with them almost immediately.

2. In team meetings, invite team members to share their hobbies or share their history. Find ways at each meeting to have them

learn something new about each other. Set aside five minutes for this exercise.

3. Have some of your employee meetings over lunch. People are always more receptive to influence over lunch than in other meeting environments. It's easier to chat amiably and share personal information over lunch.

4. In his classic book *How to Win Friends and Influence People*, Dale Carnegie suggests becoming interested in other people. This gets them to like you faster than if you spent all day trying to get them interested in you.

5. Find similarities at all costs. This is critical to building stronger relationships within your team.

Reciprocal Liking

We also tend to like those who like us and tell us so. When a person reveals to you that they like you, it's almost impossible not to like that person in return.

Think back to grade school or junior high, when boys and girls first started getting interested in each other. The boys were shy to make the first move in fear of being rejected, and the girls were shy in fear of not being pursued. Can you remember when one of your friends would come over to you and whisper, "You know, Johnny really likes you a lot"? You would glance over at Johnny, and all of a sudden he got much better looking and a little taller. You couldn't help yourself. You started to see nice qualities about him, and you started to like him better. In fact, you started to put into play your own strategies to get closer to him, and so the wooing would begin. This approach is used quite successfully among preteens, and it maintains its power over us from then on. It still works on all of us no matter our age. Had I known this secret as a young single guy, I would have been much more successful with the girls in school than I was.

Why does this simple little technique work? Why would someone you already know become more attractive simply because you are told they like you? Can influence and persuasion be this simple? It would appear that telling someone you like them influences their feelings toward you immediately.

This theory was tested by pairing college students together, and the results were outlined in the book *Social Psychology* by Elliot Aronson, Timothy D. Wilson, and Robin M. Akert. One group of paired college students were told their partner liked them, and the other groups of pairing were told that their partner didn't like them. The pairs in the "liked" group were much friendlier with each other, argued less, and cooperated more than the pairs in the groups who were told their partner disliked them. It seems obvious that we would work better with someone who likes us than with someone who dislikes us. If this is the case, why wouldn't we all simply tell those we work with that we like them? It's a mystery to me.

I was flying back from a conference a number of years ago, and I was sitting next to an older rather distinguished-looking gentleman. I was busy reading a magazine, so I didn't socialize with him that much other than a perfunctory "Hello. How are you doing? These seats aren't all that comfortable" type of thing. I wasn't looking to influence somebody at that stage of the flight.

As I was reading my magazine, I noticed an article on the ability to read foreheads. Well, this intrigued me, so I read the article. When I was finished, I turned to the man beside me and said, "Listen to this. This magazine says people can read foreheads." The look on his face indicated that he thought I was one of those people into parapsychology and other off-the-wall philosophies. Undeterred by the look, I proceeded to read part of the article. I said, "It says here that written on everyone's forehead are the words 'I want to feel important.' What do you make of that?"

Needless to say, his face again registered incredulity. He said, "There is no way that those words are written on everyone's forehead. Where are you getting your information?"

"The information is coming from a well-regarded publication on psychology and was well researched. Here. Have a look yourself."

He took the magazine and glanced at the article. He said, "Sorry, but this is completely incorrect."

"What makes you so sure? This is a very credible magazine with international circulation."

"Listen. I am a double Ph.D., and I can tell you that the words 'I need to feel important' are not on everyone's forehead."

I was a little taken aback by his credentials, so I said, "So, Doctor Doctor, what do you think this is all about then?"

"The words on the forehead are not 'I want to feel important'; they are 'I *need* to feel important.' It's a basic human need to be appreciated, and as we get older, especially with men, the letters get larger and easier to read as the forehead expands."

What this really means is we are all searching for validation. We do *need* to feel important. We need to feel we are making a contribution. We need to be appreciated. We also like people who appreciate us and tell us so. This is why a compliment is such a powerful tool in building a liking relationship.

All managers observe performance one way or another, and most managers provide feedback on performance. Since we all need to feel appreciated, look for things people are doing right and comment on those behaviours. You will discover that people will repeat this behaviour and will appreciate your management approach much more than if you always focus on what they do wrong. Helping people feel important is one of the fundamental practices of management.

Reciprocal liking is described in psychological terms as an effect whereby a person who is liked by another person will have a tendency to return that liking. The reason this works is simple. People enjoy being in the company of people who make them feel good. We all like to be with people whose company we enjoy.

B. F. Skinner was the researcher who studied and documented reinforcement and its impact on behaviour. We train animals with this method of reinforcing positive or desired behaviour using food. In humans, our needs are a little more sophisticated, but the basic principle applies. People will repeat behaviour if it's positively recognized and rewarded. A manager who thanks an employee for being creative and showing initiative will be more likely to see that employee repeat the behaviour in the future.

A compliment after an action will cause the action to be repeated more often than if not otherwise reinforced. This is an oversimplification of Skinner's work, but the basic principle of behaviourism is that behaviour can be modified using reinforcement. Reciprocal liking falls into this category. This is a powerful tool for anyone wishing to build strong relationships, and it should not be overlooked in planning your management strategies. People like people who like them first.

Compliments

Giving compliments is a proven technique to get people to like you quickly. We are suckers for flattery—all of us. The message is written on everyone's forehead. Have a look in the mirror, and sure enough, there it is: "I *need* to feel important." Anyone wishing to be influential should look at people's foreheads and pay attention to those words. They're telling you how best to influence others.

Are compliments more effective if they're true? Apparently, it doesn't matter much unless a compliment is so over the top that you feel manipulated. Otherwise, any reasonable compliment, or unreasonable one for that matter, can be quite effective.

The results of an experiment on the effects of praise were published in the article "The extra credit effect in interpersonal attraction" in the *Journal of Experimental Social Psychology*. Men were given comments about themselves from another person who needed a favour. Some of the men received only negative comments while some others received only positive comments. The rest received both positive and negative comments.

The results were quite interesting. The participants liked best the people who praised them and only gave positive comments. This was even the case when the men knew that the person providing the praise had something to gain from their liking him. It didn't matter; they liked him anyway. Finally, the positive praise didn't have to be true to be effective in getting the men to like the person providing the praise. The positive comments produced just as much liking for the provider of the praise when they were untrue as when they were true.

How do we explain this interesting aspect of human behaviour? Even when we know a compliment is false, we still like the person who provided it. We will be much more susceptible to that individual's influence. I suggest this goes back to what's written on our foreheads. We all *need* to feel important, and praise, whether true or false, seems to satisfy that need.

Another thing is that most of us feel that we are above average. Various studies have been done using secret ballots in groups to ask a simple question: Are you above average or are you below average compared to the people in this room? Statistically, 50 percent would be above average and 50 percent would be below average, but the results of these studies show that over 95 percent of the people studied believe they are above average. This is why false compliments may be just as effective as true ones. We all have a higher opinion of ourselves than reality may dictate. This is good for self-esteem and good for the manager.

In the world of management, focus your compliments on the behaviour being demonstrated rather than just the result. Managers should try to change behaviour and build on what employees do well already. Managers tend to focus on results and achievements as they compare to objectives. Compliments about these are nice, but do they really reinforce the behavioural change you're looking for?

"Good job" is not much of a compliment. Find a way to recognize what employees actually do or say to achieve a goal. Focus on behaviour. The old adage of "If you have nothing nice to say, then don't say anything at all" should be replaced with "If you have nothing nice to say, find something nice to say."

Communication

Communication problems are always referred to as the number one culprit in marriage breakdowns, but I will suggest another component that has received very little study: the words "I love you." This phrase is the most powerful likeability tool in our vocabulary. I was listening to a talk radio program recently, and they were discussing the merits of couples communicating that they love each other. The host was of the opinion that actions speak louder than words, that words were ineffective in maintaining the relationship, but actions ruled the day. Many listeners disagreed with this approach for good and valid reasons.

In management circles, actions do speak louder than words because employees watch the manager's actions for clues on how to behave and clues on what is really going on. Words are just speeches in many instances, so people rely on observation to confirm their assumptions. This works because employees don't live with their bosses; they only work for them and don't generally converse on a daily basis with the executives of a company.

Marriage is different. We live together, eat together, vacation together, and even sleep together. I suggest that there is doubt about the love the other holds for their partner in every marriage. We sometimes forget that our partner is indeed in love, and we need positive reinforcement about this on a daily basis. It's simply not enough to show your partner you love them; you must verbalize it. It seems that men in particular have a difficult time understanding this simple aspect of marriage. If you do love your partner, why wouldn't you want to tell them and tell them often? They love to hear it, and they actually love you more when you tell them.

The Exposure Effect

The more you see a person, the more likely you are to influence them. The exposure effect is characterized by the following phenomenon: The more often someone sees a certain person or product, the more pleasing and likeable the person or product becomes. It's difficult to believe, I know, but a number of studies have confirmed this. The more we see someone, the more we like them. This exposure effect is compounded by the propinquity effect, where there is a tendency for people to form friendships with whom they encounter frequently. It would appear that familiarity breeds liking rather than contempt. Things we are exposed to start to grow on us, and we develop a taste for them. When we make choices, we usually choose the familiar. "Better the devil you know than the devil you don't know" has been a hiring credo among HR professionals for years.

If you ride the subway, you can appreciate the propinquity effect. Those commuters who travel long distances on the train usually try to sit in the same seat every day, and over time, they become aware of others on the train who are doing exactly the same thing. Before long, a bond and friendship grows amongst these commuters, as they usually board the train at the same station at the same time every day.

One study entitled *Social Pressures in Informal Groups* by L. Festinger, S. Schachter, and K. W. Back followed friendships in a small apartment building. They discovered that neighbours on the same floor were most likely to be friends, and those on other floors were least likely to be their friends. The exceptions were those in apartments near the staircase and mailboxes, as they had friends on both floors.

Management by Walking Around (MBWA)

Management by walking around (MBWA) has been around for decades. Managers always knew it was a good idea to walk around the department and just see people in their natural work environment. However, as time pressures increased on managers, MBWA slipped into the background because it didn't seem efficient to just walk around and be seen in the department. It was deemed better to sit in an office and get real work done.

It seems that perhaps the real work was being done when walking around, as a manager's presence has an impact on the culture of the company. When MBWA fell to the wayside, the exposure effect became a missing ingredient to effective employees.

Going back to MBWA is perhaps why many companies shifted to open-concept offices. This allows managers to be more available and visible. Managers, always the great innovators, attempted to solve this visibility problem through the inefficiency of having more and more small meetings in rooms with doors. Managers, it's time to rethink what's important. Being with your team is critical. Start walking around!

Cooperation

We all like people who cooperate with us. Work teams produce better results when they cooperate. Cooperation is simply the practice people working together to reach an agreed-upon goal instead of working independently in a competitive environment. The success of the objective is attained through the success of all the individuals. People will say yes to a request from those with whom they are cooperating. This is why it's important to establish common goals among your team.

Who Do You Like?

Is it more important for you to like your employees or more important for your employees like you? Take a moment to think over this question. Write your answer down. It has ramifications in how we decide to proceed with the liking principle when we want to be influential and persuasive.

I have presented this question to thousands of people over the years, and the usual response is that it's better if employees like you. They reason that if people like you, they will want to work with you. At first blush, it may appear that employees who like you will be more receptive of your influence. After all, they like you and will want to please you.

A small percentage of people will think about the question a little deeper and present the option that it's better if employees know you like them.

What's the difference?

Joe Girard, one of the most famous car sales reps of all time, is recognized by Guinness World Records as the "world's greatest car salesman." For twelve years straight he won the title as the number one car salesman. He was selling Chevrolets and sold, on average, five cars and trucks every day he worked.

How could he be so consistent for so long? He had two simple rules: 1) offer the car at a fair price, and 2) let them buy from someone they liked to buy from. He is quoted as saying, "Finding the salesman they like, plus the price; put them together, and you get a deal."

What is Joe's secret to liking? He simply told people he liked them. After a client purchased a car, he would add that name to his database. Every month, the client would receive a card in the mail that had a simple message. That message was "I like you." It soon became a family tradition to buy a car from Joe. Family members all bought cars from him. They liked Joe, and they trusted Joe, and they felt that Joe liked them and they were going to get a good deal at a fair price. Liking influenced the honesty and integrity component of Joe's business. In car sales, this is quite an edge to have over your competition. Loyalty to Joe was legendary, and it all started with his two simple rules.

Notice that Joe wasn't offering the car at the *best* price, but a *fair* price. Remember, all things being equal, people will buy from those they like. It's also true with all things being unequal, as Joe's customers weren't after the best price; they were after what they saw in Joe: honesty, integrity, and trustworthiness. Joe Girard knew this and believed this and became the number one car salesman in the world.

If the employees know you like them, they will feel more comfortable that you will support them and stand up for them in difficult times. They will believe you won't hurt them in any way because you like them.

Respect vs. Liking

I have heard many managers and executives say they would rather be respected than liked. I never truly understood what they meant by this until I started to do research for this book. Employees have a difficult time respecting someone they don't like. They may respect the title of manager, they may respect your product knowledge, or they may respect your intellect, but if they don't like you, they probably don't trust you and won't follow you willingly.

It's much easier to gain the respect of employees if they like you, and this will be a winning combination. It's true that employees sometimes like a manager as a person but don't respect their management skills. I think this simply means that they don't like the manager as manager and therefore don't respect them.

As a manager, your role is to get things done through other people. People are more influenced by people they like than people they don't like. You can adjust to using the liking principle by following these simple principles and applying them to your team. Find a way to get your people to both respect you and like you.

Best Practices

1. Smile more often—life is good.

2. People need to feel important, so help them.

3. Focus compliments on behaviour, not results.

4. Find people doing things right and compliment them immediately.

5. Give compliments freely and accurately—show real appreciation for a job well done.

6. Show and tell people you like and respect them—liking is the basis of true respect.

7. Reintroduce MBWA into your management schedule.

8. Demonstrate cooperation with other departments.

Chapter 11
Consensus

Drive by any schoolyard filled with teenagers, and you will notice various groups of students gathered in small clusters. The individuals in each cluster seem to have the same taste in clothing and hairstyles, but these tastes differ from other clusters. It also seems that teens desire to be the same as each other but different from their parents. This is called peer pressure, and it doesn't just apply to teenagers but to all of us. We are social animals after all.

The principle of consensus basically states that we are influenced by what others like us are doing.

My wife and I went out for a nice dinner recently. We decided to be a bit adventuresome and tried a restaurant we hadn't been to before. We looked forward to a new culinary delight as I made a reservation for 7 p.m. on a Saturday night. We got all decked out in our finest for a nice romantic evening.

When we arrived, I noticed it was easy to park, as there were many empty spaces. How nice, I thought, I can park right by the door. We walked to the entrance. It looked lovely. We opened the door, and the place was lit with candles and soft guitar music was playing, but I noticed something amiss. There was only a waiter standing by the bar and no other patrons. The restaurant was completely empty of customers.

We just stood at the doorway and didn't know what to do next. We looked at each other. I nodded, and we turned around and headed back to the car. What would you have done in such a situation? Why did we decide to leave before we had even tasted their fare?

With no other patrons in the restaurant, we assumed the food wasn't any good. We judged the restaurant on the observation that no one else was there. If the food were great, the place would be packed, right? We were influenced by the behaviour of others. What others do or don't do influences us. We judged the quality of the restaurant by the opinion of others rather than our own.

Bandwagon Effect

When we are in a situation where we don't know what to do or how to behave, we look to others like us to determine the correct behaviour. This psychological phenomenon is called social proof. It's when we assume that others know what's going on and are behaving in the correct fashion. This becomes even more powerful when the people we observe are much like us. They look like us, they dress like us, or they work with us. Most of the time, we don't even realize this is happening, but it's a natural tendency we all have, and marketing companies take good advantage of this.

Most TV comedy shows have laugh tracks to encourage your enjoyment. We are influenced to find the show funny and laugh along with the track. The iPhone craze is another perfect example. With each new release, people line up and even sleep in front of the store locations to be the first to get the new model. The iPhone is by far Apple's most successful product, even in the wake of their now-ubiquitous iPod. The more people get iPhones, the more people want them. Since the device's initial launch in 2007, crowd mentality has influenced the masses, and sales continue to skyrocket. Today, Apple vies for the top spot as the most valuable company in the world, and much of it is because of the success of the iPhone.

We have all heard of the bandwagon effect. If someone senior has an idea, many people will agree almost immediately. As soon as a few start to agree, then more and more start to agree until it seems people are jumping on the bandwagon of the winner. This effect is rampant during elections, in sports fandom, and even in workplaces. We all know that a team gets more fans when they start to dominate the standings; we want to associate with a winner. The bandwagon effect is why books are called best sellers and McDonald's signs read "billions served." We all want to jump on the bandwagon.

The Culture

It isn't only customers who are affected by the principle of consensus; it's actually all of us. Managers rarely believe the huge impact they have on employees. The higher the level of manager or executive, the more impact they have on employees. Employees are always looking to others to determine suitable behaviour and to justify their actions. Policy and procedures only go so far in determining the company culture, so employees look to their leaders for clues. A manager who goes home early telegraphs to everyone that leaving early is acceptable. A manager's long lunches usually lead to employees having long lunches.

Employees are also influenced by what others on their team are doing. They watch each other's behaviour to help determine what's acceptable. The more the employee is liked and respected, the more influence they have. An effective manager will use this invaluable pool of resources to initiate change and improvements.

I run a workshop called "Retail Is Detail." It's the little things that most influence customer service. A clean work environment, for example, communicates a lot about a bank branch. A well-maintained branch suggests the availability of good investment advice, good interest rates, and even safety. It certainly suggests excellent service. If they care enough about the appearance, they will care as much about their clients.

To a manager who operated a branch that was a mess I suggested how to change the culture in the branch to make it tidy. Three times a day the manager would walk the floor, including the

ATM area, and pick up loose pieces of paper that were littered about. He kept his own desk and office immaculate. After only four days, he noticed fewer and fewer pieces of litter, and he noticed the teller area was tidier. He congratulated those who had tidy areas, and they got even cleaner. Soon, the worst offenders started to clean up. In a matter of weeks, the entire place looked totally different, and customers started to comment and ask whether the branch had been renovated. Business started to grow, more referrals flowed in, and everyone seemed happier. They soon received the best customer experience rating in the branch's history.

Why did this happen? The principle of consensus came into play. Once staff saw the manager's tidy behaviour, they tried it too. Once a few started, they all started because they could see that this was the proper behaviour. The manager couldn't believe the results; he had been trying for two years to get the employees to tidy the branch. Desired behaviour, once started, flowed into other aspects of their business, which lead to significant improvement.

Teambuilding

The principle of consensus works best in a team environment and can be a powerful motivator to enhance team performance or inter-team collaboration. Many companies are still in the sixties when it comes to divisional cooperation. The silo approach to structure is alive and well. Bureaucracy loves the silo mentality, which is the tendency to organize individual team units as their own disparate operational system, but how can consensus deliver team spirit and inter-team cooperation?

The key is to get initial support for your initiative from inside the team. It's like an auction house. When you attend an auction, most auctioneers have a shill in the house whose job is to bid on items so that others will see that someone else is interested and willing to pay for them. This is an unethical way to use consensus, but managers can use consensus in an ethical way to effect lasting change.

Select a small group of key employees and discuss the projected changes. Get their input, and even adjust your proposal if they have a workable solution. Obtain their commitment to the project and have several of them become team leaders to share the proposal with the rest of the team. Getting a few people on board with the project will ensure that others will view this as a good idea and will support it. When others just like them see the advantages, most will automatically agree.

The same can apply to work between two inter-department teams. Get a small group from each team to work together on a project that is critical to both teams. The smaller the group, the better—three or four people each. Any more and the session turns into another meeting, which no one wants. Keep it small, focused, and with a deadline. It may take an initial storming period before the group members will work together, but let them go to it. They will find their way through it. When they do, they will come out the other side as partners on the initiative, and that will leak into both teams. Instead of seeing each other as competitors within the same company, they will see themselves as partners, and their behaviour will change to fit the new perspective.

The Power Is Yours

The power is yours to influence team dynamics and individual performance. Cultural change usually begins to take hold when consensus takes hold. This tool is available to managers, but most of them don't think about it or downplay its impact.

Managers get things done through other people, and if you don't rely on authority all of the time, building consensus is a simple yet effective way to change behaviour. Start small to get some experience with the approach, and certainly don't use it unethically or it will come back to bite you. Consensus can go both ways: It can foster positive change or exacerbate negative behaviour.

Best Practices

1. Demonstrate daily how you want others to behave—your team will emulate your behaviour.

2. Publicly recognize those who are doing things right.

3. Get certain team members on board with your initiatives, and others will follow.

4. Set up small teams to tackle issues important to them and encourage them to make recommendations.

5. Make small changes one clear step at a time and gain momentum.

6. Be decisive yet empower your employees.

Chapter 12
Building on Strengths

In 1999, Marcus Buckingham and Curt Coffman changed the management landscape with their seminal book *First, Break All the Rules: What the World's Greatest Managers Do Differently*. Their research was based on Gallup's in-depth interviews with over 800,000 managers in more than 400 companies over 25 years. They interviewed the various companies' "best managers"—the ones everyone recognized as the key managers with an excellent reputation of accomplishment and respect from employees and peers. They also interviewed the bottom-performing managers—the ones who were mediocre at best as determined by all the normal company performance criteria. The differences between these managers is what *First, Break All the Rules* is about. The book is a must-read for every manager wishing to excel.

Prior to this book, conventional wisdom in management was to identify and document employees' weaknesses so that the company could initiate an action plan to improve these deficiencies. In my discussions with managers lately, I have found this approach is still prevalent. The Gallup research reveals that the best managers believe that people can't really change many of their personality traits and weaknesses, so it's a waste of valuable time to try to get people to make drastic "improvements." These good managers focused on the employees' strengths and built on those, and the results were significantly better than the average manager's.

One of my favourite passages from the book that I have used in many of my workshops on management and coaching is: "People don't change that much. Don't waste time trying to put in what was left out. Try to draw out what was left in. That is hard enough." This is quite a revelation for most of us. Our natural tendency is to help people get better. Even as parents, we want to help our kids become better. This leads us to look at things they are doing wrong and try to improve that. Most managers still focus on weaknesses and put together action plans to help people get better at what they are no good at. Managers seem to think that strengths will naturally take care of themselves, but the evidence suggests otherwise. It takes a tremendous amount of practice to get great at what you are already good at.

When I was a bank branch manager, I was quite successful. My strengths, which I covered on my annual performance review, were customer focus, sales focus, and an ability to grow staff skills to exceed objectives. I managed to outperform my peers most of the time and was able to move into larger and larger branches. I was good at sales and was good at getting my staff to exceed customer expectations, and we always exceeded our targets. Things were going very well for my career, and then one day the internal audit department came to audit my branch and my world changed.

If you're a sales-oriented person, you know what happened. I received an unsatisfactory audit rating, and my boss came down on me like a ton of bricks. I was put on performance standards, which basically meant that if I didn't improve, I would be fired. Apparently, the audit team had discovered my weakness, and my boss was going to make sure I focused on this and improved or I would lose my job. Needless to say, this got my attention. I did manage to pass the next audit, but this blemish on my career encouraged all future bosses to focus on my detail orientation regarding audits.

I went to courses, I was always warned about audits, and my managers encouraged me to read the manuals and to be much more conscientious about auditing. In other words, they wanted me to develop an area that I was no good at and ignore developing the areas I was pretty good at. I never got an exceptional audit review and barely squeaked by each audit, but the time I spent being control-focused limited my ability to grow the sales and service of my teams. I never got much better at what I was no good at, and I also never got much better at what I was good at until I finally left the company.

Most of us fall into this trap where the squeaky wheel gets the oil, and we disregard the true potential in front of our faces. So what should we be doing when challenged with the prospect of growing the skill sets of our employees and growing our own for that matter? Malcolm Gladwell has an answer in his book *Outliers: The Story of Success*.

Outliers

In *Outliers*, Malcolm Gladwell discusses how crucial it was for the Beatles to work hard early in their careers. "By the time they had their first burst of success in 1964," Gladwell writes, "they had performed live an estimated 1,200 times. Do you know how extraordinary that is? Most bands today don't perform 1,200 times in their entire careers." This relates to Gladwell's 10,000-hour rule, where he claims that success in any field requires practicing a skill for around 10,000 hours total. Greatness requires an enormous investment of time. The Beatles played for eight hours a day in a German strip club on their way to logging 1,200 live performances between 1960 to 1964 before they became famous. These performances amounted to over 10,000 hours of actual practice at what they did best: playing music. This explains why the Beatles are to date the best-selling music artists in history.

"The biggest misconception about success is that we do it solely on our smarts, ambition, hustle, and hard work," writes Gladwell, but a closer look reveals some interesting aspects of how to be exceptional. Gladwell points out how Lennon and McCartney had unique musical gifts. All that playing time shaped their talent until they sounded like no one else. They simply focused their energies on their strengths and devoted countless hours to honing their craft, so by the time they hit *The Ed Sullivan Show* in their introduction to North American audiences in 1964, they were already seasoned professional performers poised for greatness, and thus went Beatlemania.

Gladwell's concepts also explain why Bill Gates is a multibillionaire and one of the wealthiest people in the world. In 1968, thirteen-year-old Gates got access to a high school computer and logged around 10,000 hours of programming. Gladwell interviewed Gates, who credits his success to his luck in having that unique access. Without it, Gladwell says, Gates still would have been "a highly intelligent, driven, charming person and a successful professional"—but maybe not worth over $50 billion. Like Lennon and McCartney, Gates focused on his strengths rather than something else such as learning to play baseball or backgammon. He had an intense focus on his strengths, which included computer programming.

Professional Hockey Players

How many professional hockey players are born between January and March? Each year, an amazing statistic is revealed. More players are born in the first three months of the year than any other time during the year. This does seem strange given the fact that skills should be evenly spread out throughout the year, and yet each year, these stats remain relatively constant.

Gladwell points to research by Canadian psychologist Roger Barnsley that confirms this statistic and explains that it's the unique eligibility cut-off for age-class rules for Canadian hockey organizations on January 1st. A boy who turns ten on January 2nd will be playing in the same league as a boy who will turn ten in December. Look at the differences in a boy who is ten and a nine-year-old boy who won't be ten for another eleven months. There is a huge difference in maturity, size, and experience. When coaches choose the best players to play in the elite leagues, who do you think gets picked? That's right. The bigger, more aggressive boys who have almost a year on some of the other players.

When this happens, these boys gets better coaching, they practice twice or three times as often as other players, and they have better teammates to play with. They also get to play more games and tournaments. By the time these boys reach thirteen or fourteen, they really are better players and far more likely to make it into Junior A or a top-ranked university team. After that, professional hockey scouts come looking, and the boys born in January have a better shot at the majors.

The underlying message is that if you want your son to make it to the NHL, time his birth for January. This way he will have a much better opportunity to build on his strengths and get additional training time and playing time to move him towards that magic 10,000 hours of practice. Boys born in December may be just as talented, but they don't get the same opportunities to practice to the same degree. This reduces their chances of making it to the NHL. More practice leads to exceptional performance.

Falling in Love with Practice

Elite practitioners in any field don't just work harder than everybody else. At some point, they fall in love with practice to the point where they want to do little else. The job becomes the hobby where doing the work is fun and rewarding and hardly seems like work at all. It's almost an obsession for many of the top names in any industry. Some may even call them workaholics; however, since their work is enjoyable, rewarding, and invigorating, they can hardly be called workaholics.

The elite software developer is the programmer who spends all day pounding code at work only to write open source software on her own time. It's this commitment to practice on what she does best that leads to being an elite software developer in the first place.

The elite football player is the guy who spends all day on the practice field with his teammates only to go home to watch game films. The ones who go out and party after practice usually have shorter careers and blame everything else on their failure rather than their re-fusal to practice their profession to the degree that was required to be a world-class athlete.

Elite salespeople listen to motivational and instructional audio-books in the car in-between calls, on the drive to and from the of-fice, while doing dishes, while walking the dog, and during any other opportunity that comes their way. They know they need to continually fine-tune their game if they are to remain at the fore-front of their profession. They continually read books on sales. The average salesperson buys these books and doesn't read them; the books gather dust because average salespeople don't build on their strengths. The elites are in love with what they do, and at some point, it no longer feels like work to be continually reading books.

The professional top-tier speakers tape each presentation and spend hours fine-tuning each word and vocal inflections for maxi-mum impact. They practice continually and even give free speeches to practice new material in front of a live audience. This is the dif-ference between a $1,000 workshop and a $20,000 workshop. The difference in quality and content is obvious, and it's a result of a commitment to practice and to strive to reach those 10,000 hours.

The professional manager doesn't work 9 to 5. They take courses, read, practice their profession, and are open to coaching themselves. They practice the coaching with their employees when-ever they can. I used to even practice on my wife, but I must say this wasn't the best idea, so I gave it up and practiced on my chil-dren instead.

How much of your potential is being ignored? How much of your available talent remains dormant and finally lost because you're too busy focusing your attention on your weaknesses? You should be practicing to build your strengths instead so they become powerful enough to propel your career to the heights you deserve.

Strengths Win

The book *How to Be Exceptional: Drive Leadership Success by Magnifying Your Strengths* presents evidence suggesting that great leaders often only have three to five powerful skills that influence their performance. These three to five skills often rank in the 90th percentile and have the most impact on their company's results: "If you correlate these leaders' perceived effectiveness with employee engagement, customer satisfaction, productivity, profitability, or retention of employees—in fact, with virtually every quantifiable business outcome you can imagine—you'll find a strong connection." It's virtually impossible to elevate a weakness to this 90th percentile and turn it into a significant and fundamental strength. In reviewing thousands of development plans for leaders, the book's authors noticed a common weakness: A popular developmental target was to become a better listener. I have even had this one on mine a few times over the years. What exactly does "be a better listener" mean? There is rarely any specific behaviour attached to this development objective, and yet it appears and reappears often on managers' and executives' development plans.

As these individuals focus on cutting back their talk in conversations and avoiding interrupting others, they may improve, perhaps getting to the 75th percentile range in listening skill. They may continue this behaviour for months, but many will drift back to where they started. For most, changing this weakness into a strength and achieving a persistent 90th percentile skill level is unattainable. Let's face it. Most managers and leaders have tried to improve these kinds of weaknesses, usually noted by a supervisor, and yet building a strength is not the same as acquiring a basic skill.

The book's authors studied development efforts in one organization and rated the leaders after successive surveys in which colleagues assessed their effectiveness. Leaders who worked on their weaknesses did become more effective, moving on average from the 34th to the 46th percentile range in overall effectiveness, a 12-point gain. But leaders who built on their strengths moved on average from a 41st percentile to a 77th percentile range, a whopping 36-point jump—three times the improvement above those working on weaknesses.

In seeking to boost productivity, what approach would you take in your business and career? You can get a 12-point gain by working on your weaknesses or you can get a 36-point gain by working on your strengths. What would you do? *How to Be Exceptional* outlines several studies that clearly point to the benefits of working on strengths. The authors make the following recommendation from their research: "Concentrate on boosting your strengths, unless you have a fatal flaw that will prevent you from succeeding in your current role, whatever your gifts." The question then becomes: Do you have a fatal flaw or merely a weakness?

In my case, my lack of focus on the audit was not a fatal flaw, as I only needed minor remedial work to set up the correct systems and checks to ensure compliance. I didn't need to take my audit expertise to the 90th percentile, but I did need to improve and I did need to hire someone who was better at audit controls than me. I hired a new assistant manager who was exceptional with the details and the checks and balances, and I never had any further issues with audits. My boss, however, continually hounded me to develop my audit skills to the 90th percentile because he loved audits and that was his main focus. To him, good audits and staying out of trouble was more important than reasonable audits and growing the business.

If I were promoted to head up the audit department, then my lack of detail orientation would be a fatal flaw, and either I would be fired or the company would suffer. Needless to say, I was never promoted to head up the audit department, as I much preferred to build on strengths than develop an audit mindset that was really beyond my capacity. We can learn many things, but we can't learn everything.

Many managers and leaders still believe that you shouldn't have any weaknesses if you want to be successful. However, as *How to Be Exceptional* demonstrates, you instead need three to five powerful strengths and continually work on those. On top of that, work hard enough to keep your weaknesses from interfering with your career or your company's results. Donald Trump is a perfect example of an extremely successful person with obvious strengths that have led him to overcome adversity and come out on top. His strengths are obvious to most, but so are his weaknesses. Trump doesn't spend much time worrying about working on his weaknesses; he's too busy developing his strengths.

Think back over the path of your own career and consider some of your best bosses. I think you will agree that you can identify their strengths, because they were obvious and significant. I'm sure you can identify their weaknesses as well, but these didn't really matter much because the strengths overpowered any weakness. The success of your bosses was based on their towering strengths.

Building on Strengths

Even if you accept the premise that building on strengths is the only way to go, it isn't quite so easy to determine how to do this. First, you need to identify what your strengths are. They may include being results focused, driven to succeed, or highly competitive. Maybe you communicate powerfully, are a strong team player, or are great at developing the skills of others. If you look closely at each strength you identify, you will be able to list two or three specific behaviours or competencies for each of them.

For example, if you excel at developing the skills of others, you might have behaviours such as asking for input from others, being non-judgemental, and showing respect for the ideas of others. Once you realize what the competencies are, you can make a conscious effort to be even more inclusive with your team. You can exercise these skills and make time in your day to practice on your employees. If you want to see creativity bloom among your people, then let them go to it.

If you're results oriented, then some of the behaviours or competencies might be that you know the numbers for all your sales staff better than they do, you gain commitments from others on targets rather than dictate objectives, your leadership is enthusiastic, and you recognize performance all the time. These are just a few, and they may or may not apply to you. The key is to know your strengths and what makes them strengths and then put practices into place that will grow them.

Take humility as a core strength. Since Jim Collins identified it as a trait of successful leaders in his book *Good to Great: Why Some Companies Make the Leap... and Others Don't*, it's been on everyone's wish list. But how do you become humble? The research outlined in the book suggests the following behaviours are linked to humility: having concern and consideration for others, valuing diversity and inclusion, showing assertiveness, being open to feedback, having integrity, developing others, involving others, and being personally accountable. These are some great ideas you as a manager may want to consider in developing humility as one of your strengths.

How are you managing your strengths? Make a list of your top three to five strengths, and then get your staff to anonymously list the strengths they perceive in you. Also encourage your staff to do the same in realizing and developing their own strengths.

Best Practices

1. Be committed to practice what you love.

2. Remember, it takes 10,000 hours to master a skill.

3. Help employees discover their strengths through open discussions.

4. Always build on strengths when coaching.

5. Discover and document your own strengths.

6. Break down your strengths by listing related behaviours or competencies.

7. Refocus your energies on your strengths often.

8. Don't be tempted to improve weakness no matter how tempting.

Chapter 13
Sales Meetings

Sorry, sales managers, but the meetings most of you run are a total waste of your reps' time. I know that's a bold statement, and it may hurt your feelings, but my research says it's true far too often. Most meetings are boring and have little impact on performance.

Consider a new approach that educates, motivates, and never puts anyone to sleep. If they're looking at their smartphones with their heads down, they aren't listening to you—and it's your fault. These are salespeople full of enthusiasm, excitement, and an eagerness to make money. Normal sales meetings don't appeal to any of these three qualities, but good sales meetings can.

Sales management is slightly different from regular management, the key difference being that many salespeople work away from the office environment and are not readily visible. This makes it difficult to observe and recognize specific behaviour. Given this challenge of managing the offsite employee, I recommend a series of best practices to ensure individual and team performance. These initiatives will also apply to in-house employees as well with perhaps even more success.

There are four stages in the management of a sales force:

1. The power huddle
2. The sales meeting
3. Sales observations
4. The joint sales call

We will deal with power huddles and sales meetings in this chapter, but we will deal with sales observations and joint sales calls in the following chapter. Coaching is covered separately under the coaching chapters and may be applied to salespeople and other employees alike.

The Power Huddle

Quarterbacks use it with much success all the time—the offensive team huddles around the leader, and for each play, he outlines the expectations for the key players. The effectiveness comes from clarity of mission, carrying out appropriate activities, and the team's firm understanding of the plan and their roles in it. This unites the team in one single effort to move the ball forward. The power huddle will work for you too. It's one of the most effective leadership and management tools at your disposal, and takes just a few minutes to execute.

The power huddle is a daily five- to ten-minute team meeting held before the actual work begins for the day. In the banking business, employees gather just before the branch opens to hold a short intense meeting to agree on the actions for the day. In retail, staff members gather to get pumped before opening the store and establish a specific focus for the day. It can't be longer than ten minutes or you will lose the enthusiasm and too many priorities will arise. Your team needs only one or two specific priorities for the day. You do this each and every day.

You need to tell your team what they need to know to do their jobs—and contrary to popular belief, there are employees at all levels and all ages who want to hear those things. Employees who are disengaged feel that way because the boss isn't communicating with them. The daily huddle is a great solution, and it can work in any industry.

Dynamics of a Great Huddle

Before the workday starts, gather your team to deliver key information and align team members for the day. Be prepared with your daily focus. Are there any special events/visitors/promotions? How about a key training tip? Perhaps you could talk about production or sales targets for the day. Call centres may get commitments for a minimum number of calls or a target number of calls that lead to accounts. Focus on only one thing per huddle. It can even be how your team greets customers. Keep things simple yet always focused on your priorities. All this information gives your team direction and helps them be more productive. Remember, the goal of the huddle is short term; it's what do you want to accomplish today, not two years from now.

You also might toss in some feedback about how things went yesterday. While this is not the time to single out poor performers, you may highlight some wins from the previous day. Ask employees what the magic was for their success. Get specifics such as the actual behaviour that resulted in a win.

Make sure to ask questions and request input. If the huddle is a new concept for your team, people will be reluctant to share anything initially. Over time, however, they will see you are serious about the huddle and will work with you to make it better. Playing music to signal the beginning of a huddle works to engender excitement, and you as manager should be enthusiastic.

Always know what you're going to say before the huddle. It sets up your team for winning every day.

Why a Huddle Works

Huddles work because they're personal. You're face to face with your employees every day communicating what's important, and they're encouraged to participate. No texting or email is involved. This is direct eye-to-eye contact, still the most compelling form of communication we have. When we look someone in the eye, we know we have their attention, and we can see them understand our message. When the French toast one another, they clink glasses, looking eye to eye, a marvellous connection. The French are passionate indeed.

Engaging in eye contact shows people they're important, that you want to work with them and communicate with them. It conveys the message that you respect and trust them enough to share information with them. When you ask for their input, you're saying, "I want to hear what you have to say. I'm interested in you and the value you contribute to our team." A huddle shifts from the professional to the personal level of communication. There is no mention of "them"; it's all about "us." The huddle helps educate and align your team on key business issues while making them feel a part of the team.

When managing a sales force that's difficult to round up in the office on a daily basis, telephone huddles can work, but they aren't easy. They lack eye contact and a personal touch. A weekly huddle with your outside team is a bare minimum but should still be short—ten to fifteen minutes tops.

The Payoff

What's the payoff? You get employees who understand what is expected of them on a daily basis and who feel more connected to the team. In turn, they will work harder and will be more motivated to do their jobs the best way they know how. One of the major problems employees face is being unsure of what to do. There can be too many priorities or they can be too confusing and change too often. The huddle clarifies objectives within reach and makes meeting them much easier.

Does it always work? No. When you start the day without a huddle, you risk your team being uninformed or demotivated. Communication is one of the keys to success. FireStarter Speaking & Consulting concludes that 85 percent of their surveys indicate that communication from management is in need of drastic improvement. This is also one of the major complaints from employees on employee surveys. They don't receive enough communication in this hectic go-go work environment that is too often focused simply on results but not how to get there. A huddle will help you and your team get there. The huddle is a quick, easy, and inexpensive way to fix this major problem.

A power huddle is a short meeting with the team to gain public commitments on the day's activities and objectives. Such commitments are critical in gaining everyone's support. Once committed, they will be obliged to carry out the task and will do so willingly. These short focused meetings should be exciting, as they can be real energizers for your team. I strongly urge you to try them for at least a few months.

Sales Meetings

Sales meetings have a different function from the huddle. Sales meetings could be a half-day or all day. They tend to occur on a monthly or quarterly basis depending on geography. With quarterly sales meetings, you could have a conference call with the team between official meetings.

The purpose of the sales meeting is to get an update on progress and to determine what the sales force needs to do to ensure it hits sales targets. The numbers aspect should be concise but specific, focusing on successes and performance gaps. No salesperson wants to sit through two hours of data analysis. You will lose them after twenty minutes. Focus on the key deliverables for the team.

Along with the numbers, always discuss what went well. Find the successes and discover together what the behaviour was that led to them. Celebrate success often. For example, you could say something like, "We have exceeded our target this month in ABC sales. John, you led the company in growth. Congratulations. So, John, tell us a little bit about what you did to hit those numbers." John may downplay his behaviours and talk about being lucky. A good manager must probe deeper and gain insight into what actually caused the improved results. It may be small, but it's important to share what works. Sharing best practices is a key function of a successful sales meeting. Keep people engaged.

Skills Training

A half-day or full-day sales meeting is an ideal time to structure organized and focused skills training. One of the most common mistakes with sales meetings is trying to stuff too many items into a single meeting. Yes, you might only have a major company-wide sales meeting once a quarter or year, but you must recognize that you can't cover every topic in a single meeting. Smaller regional or district meetings can complement the annual sales meeting.

Monthly meetings with an hour or two of specific skills training or activity training is best. We want to change behaviour over time, not all in one day.

Seating

The setup of meetings is also important. Theatre-style seating encourages sleeping and allows people to avoid becoming involved. I suggest round tables with six people at each table so you can arrange smaller group discussions on certain points. Group interaction is critical in maintaining interest, especially with salespeople. Each group can tackle a key opportunity or design new scripting. When they are finished, a spokesperson from each table can share the results.

Individual feedback through personal stories is helpful and should be a part of every sales meeting. Find the performers and have them share. People love to hear from their own peer group, and besides, it gives you a chance to catch your breath. Telling stories is one of the best ways to communicate valuable information. Professional speakers always include stories to make their point because people relate to stories and can easily make the connection between a priority and the behaviour that will produce results.

The Agenda

Before finalizing an agenda for a sales meeting, consider these three key questions and ensure you have an answer for each one beforehand:

1. What is the one thing I want people to know?
2. How do I want people to feel?
3. What do I want people to do as a result of the meeting?

Obtain feedback from employees on what they would like to see on the meeting's agenda. Input from the group will ensure you don't end up doing an information dump and share a twenty-slide PowerPoint presentation on the numbers that they can't even read because they're too small. Maintain interest by including items your people want to talk about. They are the frontline of your organization and are closest to your customers. Listen and learn.

Ensure the agenda has time allocated for checking email and phones. This will reduce time spent on smartphones during the meeting and allow people to focus on the meeting when you return to business. Twenty minutes every couple of hours is usually ample.

If you're planning a team-building event, make sure it's fun. Not everyone likes bowling. Team-building sessions are often poorly received because they are poorly planned. Save your money and your time and let people go home to their family instead.

When looking at the agenda, assess the amount of "talking at you" time and then reduce it by half and spread it throughout the meeting. A two-hour lecture is a killer, and people may retain only a fraction of what you say. Kevin Higgins is president of Fusion Learning Inc., a Toronto-based sales-training firm. He was quoted in Fawzia Sheikh's article "Sales Meetings That Don't Suck," published on PROFITguide.com. "Talking *at* sales reps occupies 60 percent to 70 percent of a typical one-hour meeting," he says, during which managers spend much the time on "a product and marketing information dump." Just as bad and even more boring are status updates from various divisions within the company. Everyone wants face time with the sales group, but they have little to offer. Limit them to five minutes if you must have them at all. They can cover what's new in five minutes.

I have found that the average attention span isn't much more than ten to fifteen minutes. Each chunk of the meeting agenda should therefore never exceed fifteen minutes. Break up the action and maintain the attention span and enthusiasm for the meeting. Salespeople become more energized when they participate, so spread the participation components throughout the meeting.

The close to the meeting is just as crucial as the beginning. The team must leave on a high note and must be committed to the plans agreed upon. I have found a roundtable verbal commitment to new behaviour or activities works wonders to confirm each person's future actions. It only takes a few minutes.

Remember to review the intent of each meeting and confirm that you have answered the three key questions listed above. Following meetings, asking for feedback through a survey will ensure you will continue to grow your skills as a sales meeting leader and ensure your team is getting what they need to be successful.

Best Practices

1. Establish a regular power huddle—daily is best.

2. Keep the huddle under ten minutes for maximum impact—focus specifically on what should be done today.

3. Be well prepared in advance—you only have ten minutes.

4. Be enthusiastic in your power huddles—they should be exciting.

5. Be sure to answer the three key questions before every meeting: What is the one thing I want people to know? How do I want people to feel? What do I want people to do as a result of the meeting?

6. Get participation in your meetings—it helps keep people interested and engaged as they help find solutions to opportunities.

7. Share success, discuss opportunities, and gain commitments for action.

Chapter 14
Sales Observations

We change behaviour by observing current behaviour and making adjustments. In sales, this is done through sales observations and joint sales calls, but all managers need to observe behaviour and work with employees, whether it be on a joint sales or service call. This chapter focuses on sales, but the same principles apply to the service, manufacturing, and information industries as well.

Sales Observations

A sales observation is when a manager schedules a meeting with a salesperson during a prearranged meeting with a client. The manager's role is simply to observe the salesperson in action and take notes on the behaviour demonstrated in a live situation. The manager is not to take over the meeting, no matter how tempting it may be. The client should be informed and asked whether the manager can sit in to observe the discussion. Most clients will readily agree.

This process also works effectively when observing telephone solicitation calls, customer service interactions, call centres, and any form of staff/client interaction. The objective is to ascertain the employee's interaction skills according to your own company's customer service model or sales conversation model.

Pre-Meeting

Before the meeting, the salesperson will have completed a pre-call or pre-appointment plan. Review the plan in some detail. The plan should include the objective of the meeting or the phone call. The objective must be measurable and must move the client relationship forward. If an appointment is scheduled, the objective might be to make the sale and get another appointment for future business or make the sale and get an appointment for a follow-up meeting for additional business. The objective must be more than to just close a sale; it must focus on something else with each client interaction.

Review the rep's preparation work. What research has the rep done on this client? What does the rep know that will help take the relationship to the next level? Will it be possible to get referrals? What is the client coming in for? What other services may be of interest to this client? What might be some of the objections to the sale, and how will the rep overcome them? The rep may be nervous having the boss observe, but it gets easier with practice. The manager must provide lots of positive feedback early in the game to earn the right to come back. Both the rep and the manager should agree on how to introduce the manager to the client to ease the rep's concerns.

These are just some of the opportunities to discuss when reviewing the pre-call plan. If you don't use a pre-call plan, I strongly suggest you create one. There are thousands of different approaches, but simple is always best. My previous book *Life Is Sales* is a wonderful resource for sales-related information.

The Observation Form

Most companies have some type of sales observation form that mirrors their conversation model. Most conversation models begin with the greeting, which builds rapport to make the client feel more comfortable. Next comes the questioning phase, where the rep tries to discover and understand the client's needs. The advice stage where the rep offers solutions that fit the needs. After satisfying needs, many models try to identify another need. The process finishes up with checking for satisfaction and conducting the follow-up.

The observation form should have each of the headings appropriate to your model. There should be space for the manager to note the actual words used in the meeting and to rank the performance of each section.

Sales Observation Checklist

	Did well	Next time
GREETING		
Uses client's name in intro		
Builds rapport		
Finds a similarity		
Checks to proceed		
UNDERSTANDING		
Open-focused questions		
Listening skills		
Restatements		
Narrowing questions		
Discovers the true need		
Provides advice around a solution		

	Did well	Next time

CLOSE

Provides advice

Asks for the business

Gains a commitment

Closes the sale

Discovers other needs

Goes back to understanding needs

Provides advice

Closes secondary need

SATISFACTION

Checks for satisfaction

Asks for a referral

Sets another appointment

Thanks client

Client talked more than half the meeting

This is a sample form that covers some of the key ingredients in a successful sales conversation. You can include your own conversation model in the matrix. The simplicity of the form itself is what counts. Keep the observation process simple and focused on what the rep says and does. The effective use of this form will allow for rewarding discussions after each observation.

Taking Notes

Taking notes is an important part of your role as observer. The objective is to note the actual wording used in the various components so you can discuss them in detail during the debriefing. You are looking for things that went well. What specific behaviour did the rep demonstrate that helped the sales process? Did they meet expectations around the greeting and the check to proceed? What open-focused questions did they ask? How did they restate things to encourage more conversation from the client? How did they provide advice? Did they ask for the business or just hint at it? Did they ask for a referral? What words were used?

In each section, your comments may simply be a yes, but they'll often be something more specific. You can't solve all issues in one observation, so you should focus your attention on one area and provide detailed notes on what you observed.

There are going to be areas where the rep failed, so you should document what was said that resulted in a missed opportunity. Again, noting the actual words is important. The goal is to change sales behaviours, so the details are important to clarify what reps are doing well and what they could do better next time.

Many managers in my experience decide to focus on only one of the sections of the conversation model at a time because they don't often have the time to sit through the entire meeting with clients. I think this is fine, especially with the first two quadrants of the model. The greeting and rapport building can be first, and the manager can leave after documenting this process. The debriefing can occur after the client has left, and you will have an opportunity to build on strengths regarding this section of the model. This approach serves two purposes. First, it saves the manager time, which creates more opportunities to cover more salespeople more frequently each month. Second, it allows the salesperson to focus specifically on one area at a time and become better in phases. People learn better with specific focused practice.

The Debriefing

Immediately after the meeting is the best time for the debriefing or the sales observation coaching session. The normal coaching guidelines apply to this exercise, which are covered in the coaching chapters.

I remember one coaching session I experienced many years ago. The manager's first words out of her mouth were, "Well, that didn't go so well, did it?" I slumped in my seat a bit, cast my eyes to the floor, and picked some lint off my jacket. These few words shifted my perspective to focus on all things I had done wrong rather than try to build on my strengths. Perhaps I had no strengths, and this was to be the end of my career.

The objective of the debriefing is to build on what went well. Have the rep pull out the pre-call plan while you ready your notes. Your first words should be, "Did you meet the objectives of our pre-call plan?" After a discussion on the results, move on to ask, "What went well with the appointment?" It's important to have the rep tell you what went well first. This is often difficult, as most of us tend to focus on what went wrong, but you must persist.

For each accomplishment outlined, the manager must drill down to discover what the rep said and what skills the rep demonstrated. This reinforces successful words and effective skills that helped in the rep's success. Discuss specific words that had an impact and moved the conversation forward to a successful close. These are your observations, which will be different from what the rep talked about. Discussing skills is important, as it sets the stage for improvements. The rep may have used skills regarding initiative, persistence, or listening. Find the skills and discuss them.

Now we move into next time. Ask the rep what they could do next time to be more successful. Discuss the words and the actions. Have them pick only one. You then share your observation and again pick only one (or two at the most) to focus on improving until the next sales observation.

Commitment

Once the debriefing is done, it's time to focus on the commitment for improvement. At this point, you have identified an area that will get some fine-tuning. Ask the rep how they can improve the skill they've chosen to focus on. It may be asking for referrals. Get a commitment from the rep that they will ask for a referral from the next client that day and review what words they will use.

Once you gain the rep's commitment to use the most effective words, you're done. Thank the rep for the opportunity to review their work. Communicating that you agree with the commitment confirms it. Leave on a positive note of encouragement.

Joint Sales Calls

Joint sales calls are when you accompany a salesperson on a call to participate in the discussion. The call may be to a referral source or an actual customer. It's a great opportunity for the sales manager to connect with referral sources and demonstrate how important they are to the company. It also provides a unique opportunity to demonstrate the right behaviour or a specific skill to a client.

Referral sources always want to be appreciated. Introducing them to the manager is always welcomed and often leads to immediate business. This is an opportunity for the manager to share a wider vision of the company and the value proposition to clients. You must be able to add some value to the relationship with your presence, whether it's a new insight into the business, a stronger relationship, or helping introduce a new product line.

You will be observing the rep in action, but it's not necessary to take notes, as this isn't a true sales coaching opportunity. In the pre-call plan, you will be able to establish objectives for both of you during this meeting. It's not a social call; it's a business call. Both you and the rep should have definable objectives for this meeting.

The Debriefing

After the sales call, you and the rep can discuss what went well for both of you. Did you achieve your objective? If not, what could you do differently next time to achieve it? Did you get a commitment?

Engage in a discussion of when to do the next joint sales call, and commit to building on the relationship and on your strengths. With the debriefing, there is a tendency to talk about the client or referral source versus talking about the rep's skills. Allow the rep to get their thoughts out about the client quickly and formulate the next steps they should follow. Next, refocus the discussion on the rep and their skills. This is a skill-building exercise, not just a conversation about the client and the results of the meeting. Gain a commitment from the rep to hone a specific skill or to repeat a strength and build on it to increase sales. Small improvements every time add up to significant gains over a year.

In the retail and service industries, a joint sales call could be as easy as the manager introducing themselves to a client when engaged with an employee and then sticking around for the conversation and contributing where necessary. It doesn't have to be formal every single time. This is, a learning and development process that will work in many different ways. It won't work, however, if you never do it.

Best Practices

1. Have a pre-call plan and review objectives with the rep.

2. Preparation is the key to a successful meeting—review prep notes on the client or referral source.

3. The intention should include a rep's skill focus and an outcome for the client interaction.

4. Have a scheduled appointment to attend and agree on how to be introduced.

5. Take extensive notes documenting the exact words used.

6. Look for things that are working and document those.

7. Follow a disciplined process of observing the points of your sales model.

8. Bite your tongue—you are observing specific skills, not talking.

9. Debrief by first asking what went well—provide positive feedback.

10. Tell what went well with specific words from your notes.

11. Don't talk about what went wrong.

12. Try to schedule sales observations at least monthly.

13. Gain a commitment for improvement from the rep for each observation.

14. End with a specific action plan for the rep's skill practice.

15. In the following observation, review the previous action plan, gauge progress, and provide positive feedback.

16. Use joint sales calls to help build the business and the rep's skills and strengths.

Chapter 15
Who to Coach

When looking at the performance of your employees and the overall team, where do you look first to improve the overall results? If you're like most managers, you have a tendency to look at the bottom half of performers and think, "If I could only move them up to the middle, we would experience an excellent growth year." The top performers are doing really well, so you don't want to interfere with their already excellent performance. I have seen this philosophy used in sales organizations and service companies countless times. Is this the right approach?

I recently heard several sports announcers discussing the Los Angeles Lakers basketball team and lamenting their performance. Their suggestion to the coach was to focus the coaching energy on those players averaging less than 4 points a game, as Kobe Bryant, perhaps the best player in the game today, was carrying the team with an average of 30.5 points a game. "Just leave Kobe alone. He's doing fine without any help. Get those deadbeats on the bench to contribute and win some games" was the common refrain on the radio.

Even in sports, they want coaches to focus on the weakest players and leave the winners alone. In sales, managers focus on the underperformers to help them contribute more to the team's growth. In banking, managers focus attention on the underperforming branches to get them up to par with the high-performing branches.

The thought process seems to make sense: If we could get underperformers to perform, all would be good. But how easy is it to get underperformers to perform? Even if we could get them to perform, is this the best use of scarce time resources?

It's All in the Percentages

If you could guarantee a 10 percent performance increase in any player through coaching, but you only had time to coach half the players, who would you coach? Would you still coach the bottom performers? In the Lakers' situation, coaching a 10 percent improvement in the bottom performers with an average of 4 points a game would increase their production to an average of 4.4 points per game. If you decided to coach Kobe Bryant instead, a 10 percent improvement would yield an average of 33.6 points per game.

The math is quite simple. Coaching a bottom performer in this case would lead to an average gain of 0.4 points per game. Coaching the top player, on the other hand, would lead to an average gain of 3 points per game. Focusing your energies on the top performer would have an impact 7.5 times greater than focusing on a bottom performer, and when a single 3-point basket can make or break a game, this difference is significant.

So why do we continually focus our energies on the weakest rather than the strongest? Our natural tendency is to want to be helpful, so we focus on weaknesses rather than strengths. We believe we can fix the weaknesses and deliver superior performance, while believing the superior performer doesn't need much help. This couldn't be further from the truth.

Coach the Best First

With limited resources, you must choose where to spend your energies. Shifting your priorities to your best performers will yield better results. Part of the challenge lies in employees' perceptions of coaching. Some see coaching as a negative consequence to underperformance, so they are understandably reluctant to be coached. Coaching must be seen and perceived as a compliment to performance and a contributor to personal growth. Many top performers in most businesses actually pay for a coach themselves because they know it will help them excel. Top athletes who are already exceptional usually have more than one coach. As managers, we often feel that star performers have earned the right not to be coached because they are already top performers. Even when Tiger Woods was ranked the number one golfer in the world for over five consecutive years while he owned every tournament, he still practiced with a golfing coach.

Some employees may have a performance gap related to a skill that requires training rather than coaching. For new employees, training and becoming competent should be your number one priority. These may be training opportunities instead of coaching opportunities, but they're another use of resources within the company to address skill gaps. This is why it's important to focus coaching energies where it counts. You must use limited resources wisely.

Below are the types of employees that most managers can relate to:

Star performers are employees who regularly exceed expectations. They're always improving and could almost certainly handle tougher assignments. They have a high degree of skill and exert tremendous personal effort in their role.

Solid performers usually meet—and sometimes exceed—expectations, but they're at or near their capacity and probably couldn't handle tougher work. They're often newer employees who try hard and put in the effort, but they lack the experience and knowledge necessary to be "star performers." With additional training and motivation, these employees are primed for coaching and are your best candidates to become stars. It is their effort that separates them from the other two quadrants.

Poor performers rarely, if ever, meet expectations. They can't perform their current tasks adequately, and they certainly can't handle more difficult work. This group has basic skills, and they don't demonstrate much personal effort to improve. They're often classified as lazy. They're probably in the wrong job.

Underachievers are those who sometimes meet the requirements, but their work is not what it could be. With the right skills, or the right motivation, they could do far greater things. They experience bursts of performance, so we know they have the talent and the ability to apply it, but they lack the continual effort or the full range of skills to put it all together into practice all of the time.

The Performance Grid

EFFORT

Underachievers	Star performers	S K I
Poor performers	Solid performers	L L

This chart uses two criteria to assess performers. Does the employee have the skill to do the job? Do they put in the effort to do a great job? The answer to these two questions will place the employee somewhere on this grid. This will assist you in managing them. Is skill training required? Behavioural training? Do they have a motivational issue? Motivation is important. Those who put in the effort are the ones to coach first, as they are the most receptive and will give the biggest payback.

The temptation for average managers is to leave the star performers alone to achieve greatness on their own. This is based on the assumption that they're doing just fine. They ignore the underachievers for being a common source of frustration. They will, however, spend time with the solid performers because it's the easiest. Finally, they spend far too much time with poor performers in the hopes of improving them.

This approach wastes too much time and fails to achieve the greatest impact possible through coaching. Imagine a vertical line down the centre of the chart above. This is the great coaching divide. In world-class organizations, the greatest return on the investment of time is in coaching star performers and those who have the potential to become star performers. Great coaches focus on the two right quadrants because that is where the payoff lies. Choose the ones who put in the effort on their own, and they will outperform those you have to continually push to put in the effort.

The two left quadrants need to show they are capable of putting in enough effort before they receive significant coaching. I know it isn't easy, as our natural tendency is to focus on underperformers. We all look for performance gaps and then try to fill them by working with employees of all kinds. The self-starters should be the ones you focus on.

Best Practices

1. Train skills to adequate proficiency before coaching.

2. Coach your best performers first and often—the biggest payoff comes from those who show the effort.

3. Remember that coaching is a benefit to employees, not a penalty—the best employees want coaching more than poor performers.

4. Poor performers should show they are capable of putting in the effort before you coach them.

5. Categorize your employees using the performance grid.

Chapter 16
The Coaching Process

Coaching is necessary to grow the skills of employees and change behaviour to match corporate priorities. So how do we coach in a way that yields the greatest results within the right amount of time? Many coaching programs are too time-consuming for the busy manager and are designed to cover way too many things in each session. Most companies find that the coaching results slowly dissipate over time. Coaching programs are also often replaced with the next flavour of the month.

Managers are inundated with shifting and changing priorities all the time. The goal remains the same: getting things done through other people. What gets done changes from time to time, but working through other people doesn't. So let's look at a simple process that gives managers the flexibility and discipline necessary to change behaviour over time.

Timing

An effective coaching program should be delivered on a consistent basis. Many companies have a weekly coaching session, but most are either every two weeks or once a month. Every week is best for new employees, as they need to define their skills and learn new behaviours that will lead to success in as short a time as possible. After six months, you can reduce the schedule to every two weeks. Monthly isn't often enough to obtain the kind of behavioural change you're looking for. Every two weeks provides continuity and consistency to the messages.

An effective coaching session can be as short as twenty minutes, but it shouldn't exceed a half hour. Longer is rarely better, as your employees can only absorb and agree to so much. We all have a limit. Under a half hour seems to force both manager and employee to focus on the things that matter and only those things.

Skills

The employee should speak more than the manager in an effective coaching session. Coaching dialogue is intended to encourage the employee in self-discovery. They need to learn what their skills are and how to apply them to the areas that will lead to more effective performance. The right skills enhance the right behaviours, and this leads to enhanced results. Focus on the skills and behaviours that count.

Pinpointed Behaviours

Part of the success of coaching is the practice of the right pinpointed behaviours. The manager and the employee may define the right behaviour before focusing on it until it is quite specific and can be easily observed and monitored. This behaviour could be as simple as asking for a referral. This would be the activity: Ask for a referral during each client appointment. The pinpointed behaviour then focuses on how to ask and when to ask for the referral. What do you say? Below is a sample of a coaching planner that will help with this.

Coaching Planner

Name   **Date**

Preparation

Objective from the Last Coaching Session

1.

2.

3.

Manager's Notes	**Employee's Comments**
Agenda for the Coaching Session	Results from the Last Coaching Session
Ask what went well	
Tell what you thought went well	
Ask what could be done more effectively	
Tell what could be done more effectively	

Agree on new objectives for next time

1.

2.

3.

Next coaching date

Signature   _____

This is just a sample form. You can easily design your own that fits with your company's approach. There are hundreds of designs available on the Internet if you do a search for "coaching planners." We will go through each section above to clarify the purpose and how to complete them.

Preparation

Before the coaching session, review the previous coaching planner document to confirm the objectives and move them to the new form for this session. Also gather any observation forms you may have completed on the employee. You can use this information to add to your comments about strengths and areas for improvement.

You will have confirmed the date and time of the coaching session and gained the employee's commitment that they will be prepared to attend. You will have reviewed any pertinent numbers relative to their performance and documented successes and performance gaps for discussion.

On your planner, document one strength and one development issue you would like to focus on. Consider how you will build on the strength as applied to the development area. Make a note about what you would like the employee to commit to and how will you gain that commitment. Can you think of any objections that may be raised by the employee? If so, be prepared to deal with it.

The employee will be prepared by having their copy of the coaching planner completed. This includes the last coaching session's action plans and their comments on their achievements. They will take the time to think about their performance against these action items and come prepared to identify what they did well and how they could be more effective.

Objectives from the Last Coaching Session

Both you and the employee complete this section of the form before the meeting. On the right side, each of you provides results against the specific action plans or objectives.

Agenda for the Coaching Session

Outline today's agenda for the employee and then ask if they would like to add anything to it. The agenda will include the coaching session but could also include any areas of interest to either party. Items such as future training, upcoming campaigns of interest, holiday schedule, special results of an area not included in the day's objectives, or any topic of interest at that time. Once you and the employee agree on the agenda, you're ready to move to the next section.

Results from the Last Coaching Session

Both parties would have documented their results of the action items agreed to last time. A short review of the results is appropriate as long as there is no discussion about why things happened. This will occur next.

Ask What Went Well

The notes on your form should confirm what went well since last time. The employee should complete this section from their perspective. You may say something like, "I see we hit this objective. Tell me what you did well to achieve this result." Your goal is to ensure that the employee explains what they did well in their own words. This is a moment of self-discovery as the employee tells their boss something they did well. We don't often get the chance to brag.

If the employee starts to talk about what went wrong, redirect the conversation back to the positives. This is not the time yet for you to talk, so don't take over the discussion. Be patient and let them tell you in their own words. As they describe an event, look for activities and behaviours that led to the result. Try to isolate a skill or words they used. It may help to say things like, "Tell me a bit more," or "What words did you use?" This is the most critical part of coaching as you try to determine the employee's strengths so you can both build on them.

If you can help the employee define a specific skill they demonstrated, all the better, as the employee can hone the skill and become more effective over time. Try to get two or three very specific things they did well this coaching period. They should have documented at least one on their form.

As the employee speaks, you should make notes on the right side of your form. Provide positive feedback on the things they say to encourage a more open dialogue.

Tell What You Thought Went Well

Now it's your turn to talk. Tell the employee what they did well by your observations. Refer to your notes so the employee knows you have taken the time to prepare. You might say something like, "I noticed that you showed some real persistence with Mr. Jones by asking him twice for a referral. On the second request, he said okay. Nice work on not giving up the first time. In sales, persistence is an important part of success, and I was delighted to see you give it a second try. It worked. Congratulations. I noticed that you asked for a referral from a family member the second time, and he had one for you. The more specific request for the referral is what worked."

Try to have several positive comments about the employee, and refer to the success of any action items from last time. Be specific by referring to the employee's actual words or describing their actual activities. A comment from your last observation would be appropriate as well. Maybe you have a compliment from a customer you could share. Make sure you identify the skill that led to the compliment. This is a joint effort to showcase the behaviour and/or skill that resulted in success. This can be applied later in the developmental discussion.

Ask What Could Be Done More Effectively

Once you have dealt with strengths and skills, it's time to move to the developmental stage. Again, it's critical that you ask first rather than tell. We want the employee to decide on the developmental area. This will ensure a stronger commitment. Simply say, "You had some excellent results. Let's talk about what you can do more effectively to continue this improvement." The employee will usually have something to say, but it's often not too detailed or specific. A good manager drills down with questions to help the employee discover the real development issue. Many people have trouble asking for the business, so let's use that as an example:

Employee: "Well, I don't seem to get the second piece of business or a referral too often, so I guess I could do that better next time."

Manager: "What gets in your way of getting that second piece of business?"

Employee: "I forget to ask sometimes, but I will do better next time."

Manager: "You forget?"

Employee: "Yeah, I have trouble remembering to ask, and I usually get a no from most people anyway, so I don't really ask too often."

Manager: "What are some of the consequences of not asking for referrals?"

Employee: "First off, I guess I don't get many referrals if I don't ask, but I feel I'm intruding on the client if I ask too boldly. I mean, I don't like to give referrals myself."

Manager: "So by not asking, you don't get referrals, but the reason why you don't ask is because you think the client won't like it and will say no."

Employee: "That's right. I haven't earned the right to ask yet."

Manager: "How could you earn the right to ask?"

Employee: "Well, I guess if I did a great job in providing advice, and they were really happy, then I guess I could ask those clients because they know me and I know them."

Manager: "How often do clients tell you that they're pleased with your service and advice?"

Employee: "Probably half the time, as I do work hard to give my clients the best advice."

Manager: "Yes, I know you do great work, and your clients know it too. Given what we just talked about, what will you do in the next two weeks that will increase referrals?"

Employee: "I get your point. I will ask every client for a referral who thanks me for doing a great job and providing helpful advice."

Manager: "Let's write that one down as one of our commitments for our next session. I like this commitment to focus on customers who trust you and to whom you have delivered exceptional advice. How do you feel about asking these clients for a referral now?"

Employee: "It's a start. I will work on it during the next two weeks. I will get ten new referrals in two weeks, which is four times as many as I usually get."

Manager: "Excellent. Let's write that expected outcome down in our goal section. This is a great way to measure your success."

This simple dialogue takes less than five minutes, and yet this manager helped the employee discover an issue that is holding them back. Through self-discovery, the employee found a solution that works for them and moves them forward. The manager identified that the employee doesn't feel they have earned the right to ask for a referral, so they decided to zero in on clients who receive great advice. This helps the employee's confidence in asking, and they will get a yes more often.

It's important for the employee to have success, as it reinforces the desirable behaviour. Telling the employee to ask everyone won't work because they will face too much rejection, which may lead to avoiding asking at all. By focusing on a strength, it will be easier to implement the changed behaviour and the employee will have more success. Building on success and focusing on clients who like the employee will make the transition easier.

We don't need to solve all of the problems in one day, but we can move certain skills and behaviours forward every coaching session. Be patient and talk out the issues, but don't take the problem as yours and fix it for them. Many managers want to fix problems by dictating solutions. This only works in the short term when what you want are long-lasting behavioural changes. Self-discovery and building small wins leads to locking in behaviours for better results.

Tell What Could Be Done More Effectively

Now it's your turn. Refer to your notes and talk about the one development issue you would like addressed. Refer back to the pinpointed behaviours for the coaching session or the objectives. An issue might be attempting to close the sale too soon rather than staying in the understanding stage long enough. Many in sales try to be an order taker rather than an advisor. You might say, "Today I would like to focus our attention on the understanding stage of the cycle. Tell me how you use open-focused questions in your discussions with your clients." This will lead to a discussion, and through self-discovery the employee may realize they don't use enough open-focused questions in their client interviews. This may be the time for a quick role-play or a referral back to your observation notes to discuss what was said. This opens the door for discussions on what could be said. A good opener would be, "What are the consequences of not learning enough about your customer needs?"

Once an agreement is reached to ask more questions, you could drill down to three specific questions that will be practiced over the next two weeks. Write these down as part of the employee's commitment to the coaching. Take one good development opportunity, and that's enough.

Another approach is to discuss one of the employee's strengths. Perhaps the strength is expert product knowledge and a keen desire to help people. A good question might be, "How can you use your strong product knowledge and your desire to help people when uncovering clients' full needs as you work towards providing quality advice?" Employees will usually answer such questions with what you need to hear. This is their commitment to work on their questioning skills.

Dealing with Bad Behaviour

Sometimes the coaching session will need to deal with disruptive, inappropriate, or unsuccessful behaviour. We can call it bad behaviour, but usually it's just the wrong behaviour for the circumstances or opportunity. Many managers refer to this as a bad attitude. It's difficult to change a personality; it's much easier to change a behaviour. Behavioural change will solve the problem and eliminate the so-called bad attitude.

Let's take the issue of talking to other staff when customers are present. Customers, managers, and other staff find this behaviour disruptive. You will have to deal with this behaviour during the coaching session. Will you simply demand they stop talking during business hours? Will you penalize them for talking too much? Will you reward them if they stop talking too much? There are many options that that I'm sure most managers have tried. Coaching offers the best long-term solution.

First, get the employee to realize the consequences of talking and gossiping in front of customers. The best way to do this is through self-discovery. Have them discuss various ways of dealing with the behaviour and its consequences. What strengths do they have that they could apply to this situation to adjust behaviour? What could the employee be doing to reduce the opportunity for gossip? There are many different approaches to try as long as they are the employee's choices and they commit to the new agreed-upon behaviour. Gaining a commitment is far better than demanding the employee to change.

Agree on New Objectives for Next Time

This is where the rubber meets the road—the actual commitment stage where people promise to do something. As we know, if someone makes a promise, they will work hard to keep it.

These objectives should not all be results-oriented. The purpose of coaching is to change behaviour or change activities. If the objective is a result, you must also identify the attendant behaviour that will help achieve it. It's important that the employee write these objectives on their planner in front of the manager. The manager will also document these objectives on their own copy. People live up to what they write down.

It's All in the Detail

We know we can't achieve perfection on the first coaching session, so we want to catch the employee doing something right and move them towards the overall objectives. If the objective is to get ten referrals, you need to focus on the activity and behaviour that will help the employee reach that number. The long-term goal may be to get referrals from half of all client appointments. In this case, the employee will need to practice the right behaviours and make them a part of their day-to-day performance. Telling them to do it won't work.

Outlining specific details will bring action to life, which takes the objective out of the theoretical realm into the possible and attainable. A targeted number of outbound phone calls is a common objective in many companies attempting to find new clients. An objective I often see is, "I will make more outbound calls." This has no real meaning and is therefore no help in achieving good results. If a manager says the team "needs more calls," each team member is on their own to get them. How likely will the manager see improved performance?

Great managers come up with specific and attainable objectives. They will determine exactly how many calls would be a good target for a particular employee. They set an actual number, and now the focus becomes, "What new behaviour can you implement to achieve this objective?" Perhaps together the manager and employee can decide to focus on customers who made a purchase in the past six months. They can verify the satisfaction of these customers and get appointments from 20 percent of these calls. They can determine the best time to call and how many calls to make per day. This objective is specific, and detailed behaviours and activities that fit the situation will lead to good results. You can take this further by scripting the phone call and role-playing with the employee until they become comfortable with it. The script then becomes the behaviour.

The next coaching session can build on successes and ask more from the employee. Over the course of a few coaching sessions, the focused behaviour becomes a strength that can be developed further and used in other parts of the job. Test the actions that arise out of the behaviour to ensure they move the employee in the right direction towards established objectives.

When agreeing on objectives, be as specific as you can. It helps clarify expectations, which leads to doing the right things. Confusing or misleading expectations lead to doing the wrong things or doing nothing useful at all.

Achievable Objectives

I had a manager once who believed that if we set targets for the stars, the employees would hit the moon. He wanted huge targets that were unattainable because he felt this would make employees try harder and therefore perform better. I believe there are many managers who believe in this same strategy. Is this the right approach?

This manager also believed that if objectives were within reach, employees would stop producing if they reached them before year-end. He had little faith in his employees' natural desire to excel, preferring to think of them as lazy and unmotivated once they reach targets. While there may be some employees who play this game, I believe they are in the minority.

In his book *IBM: How the World's Most Successful Corporation Is Managed*, David Steuart Mercer recounts how Thomas J. Watson, the founder and president of IBM, believed in the capacity of the human spirit, as did his son Thomas J. Watson, Jr., who was president until 1971.

Thomas Jr. believed that if you set realistic goals, people would exceed them and be motivated to produce even more. This is a big difference in perception from my former manager. Under Thomas J. Watson, Jr., IBM launched one of the most successful and recognizable sales teams in American history. He ensured that goals and objectives were set so that 80 percent of employees could achieve them. The results were astounding, as success built upon success and IBM became the company of choice for graduates from across the world. The pride of accomplishment built a confident and skillful team that led the world.

A great manager wants employees to succeed. Finding employees doing something right is easier if they can achieve specific targets. The personal satisfaction of achieving objectives encourages reaching for more success. For example, once a child learns how to ride a bike, they don't stop riding; they keep on going. Winning at something is fun and rewarding, whether it's learning to ride a bike or reaching a sales target. Give your employees the chance to be successful.

Next Coaching Date

After completing the coaching session, do a quick debriefing and ask the employee what they liked about the session. I have discovered in my research that if you don't tell people you're actually coaching, they don't think it's coaching. They seem to think it's an update or a discussion. It's important that employees appreciate that this is coaching in action. This clarifies for the employee the value of coaching and reinforces the relationship. They will usually say something nice, and when they say it, they have a tendency to believe it. This is good for the coaching relationship. Thank the employee for their time and tell them one thing you liked about the coaching session yourself.

At this point, you will have just completed the new objectives segment. Review the objectives and ensure they're documented on both your form and the employee's. Have the employee repeat the new objectives and say they will achieve these by the next session.

Next, set an appropriate date for the next session that is mutually convenient. Confirm what the employee will bring next time. This formality at the end adds credibility to the importance of the coaching process and demonstrates your commitment as a manager to the employee's growth and career.

After the Coaching Session

Once the employee leaves your office, make a few notes on how you felt the coaching session went. Simply jot down your impressions on the employee's strengths or areas that you want to build on in future coaching sessions. This documentation is important if you're coaching several employees. Coaching is a disciplined business, and your notes will help you keep on track and keep building toward your goals.

These notes will form the basis of your annual performance review where you assess employees relative to their peers and the company determines salary increases and bonuses if appropriate. The actual documentation is an important part of the review process, and when you complete them in detail, it will ensure accuracy and save time during the hectic period around performance appraisals.

Over the next several days, find opportunities to chat with employees and communicate your level of satisfaction with the coaching process. Take the time to find them doing something right relative to their new objectives established during their coaching sessions. Reinforcing their behaviour after coaching sessions adds to the stickiness of the targeted behaviours. Your employees will feel good when they learn they're doing something right and moving in the right direction. This is good news for changing behaviour over time.

Best Practices

1. Coach your employees at least every two weeks.

2. Keep coaching sessions to twenty or thirty minutes maximum.

3. Plan ahead for the coaching session by using a coaching planner.

4. Choose pinpointed behaviours that are specific and detailed.

5. Always ask first and then tell.

6. Document discussions and note strengths that employees can build on.

7. Use strengths to apply to areas that could be improved.

8. Focus on four strengths to one area for development.

9. Help employees outline strengths and areas of development through self-discovery.

10. Encourage employees to choose their own objectives for the next coaching session.

11. Ensure objectives are specific behaviours or activities.

12. Follow up with employees after coaching sessions and find them doing things right to reinforce pinpointed behaviours.

Chapter 17

Feedback: The Breakfast of Champions

When I was a manager, I experienced what many now call "constructive" feedback. I was presenting a sizable loan application to the VP for approval. I thought it was a clean deal, and I had prepared all the documentation that I felt necessary to gain approval. The VP glanced at the deal, looked up at me, and said, "Why would you present this credit application to me? It's the worst proposal I have seen in ten years. Do you even know what good credit looks like?" I was stunned by the anger in his voice and shrunk down in my chair. I felt like a whipped puppy and didn't know what to do next. He threw the credit application at me and said, "Don't bring me any more garbage deals like this."

This "constructive" feedback focused on what I had done wrong and can correctly be classified as negative feedback. I still didn't know what I had really done wrong or how to do it right. I slinked out of the office personally devastated. My credit approvals started to decline because I was afraid to face the criticism again. This type of situation may not happen often, but there is tremendous power in feedback—power to grow, and power to wither.

My VP confused feedback with criticism, and many managers

do the same. Much of our experience with feedback has had more to do with what we've done wrong than what we've done right or how we could do better. This is unfortunate. Feedback should not be viewed as a personal assault or a list of errors or mistakes. While the content of the feedback can be perceived as negative, its delivery must always be constructive. If it's not, the feedback won't be accepted and may be received as an insult or personal attack, which can ignite other issues and problems. Constructive feedback handled effectively is perhaps the most motivational management tool we have. It provides encouragement, support, corrective measures, and clear direction. It doesn't get much better than that.

Why Feedback Is Important

The main reason we provide feedback is to help the people improve. Feedback is crucial to an organization's ongoing development and growth. The key to constructive feedback in the competitive business environment is this continuous improvement. Feedback encourages all of us to build on strengths or to fine-tune our approach.

There are two types of feedback: positive and constructive. Positive feedback is designed to encourage individuals to repeat certain behaviour and make it even more effective. It's inspirational and motivating. Constructive feedback is designed to discourage or eliminate certain behaviour and replace it with more effective behaviour.

In sports, players will watch game videos for feedback on their performance, and they will observe what they did well and determine what areas could be improved on. If they were to focus only on the areas that need attention, they would have an erratic approach to improvement, as each game reveals different areas of improvement. Instead, they focus on key strengths to build on and specific areas for improvement that they stick with until they too become strengths. In football, the quarterback may notice opportunities where he could have run the ball instead of passing. Should he focus his attention on his running game or his passing game? If he focuses too much on running, he may well have a short career.

It's really why they keep score in all sporting events. The feedback is immediate and significant. Can you imagine a professional sporting team that doesn't keep score? Can you imagine playing golf and not counting your strokes? The score informs the players of things that are working that should be repeated and informs of the things that need attention. The coach's job is to define the behaviour that works and the behaviour that doesn't. Feedback is how we improve and grow.

I remember as a young man cutting the grass—it was always a great pleasure—and then sitting up on the porch, sipping a beer, and looking out to see what I had done. That's immediate feedback. Painting the kitchen provides immediate feedback with each stroke of the roller. I find these therapeutic and good lessons on the power of positive feedback. They encouraged me to do more of the same. One of my favourite things to do to relieve stress is ironing. That's right. I love to iron wrinkly cotton shirts. It's the immediate positive feedback I get with each stroke of the hot steaming iron. I look down and see the wrinkly sleeve of my shirt. I swipe the iron across it and the wrinkles magically disappear. The positive feedback says I did something right, so I do it again and again. With each pass of the iron, I calm down and focus on the beauty of a smooth cotton shirt, and the behaviour is reinforced and repeated. This is the power available to all coaches. Find the wrinkles and smooth them out, and you will achieve your success.

What to Do

If you want your employees to agree that you give meaningful positive feedback on a regular basis, do the following:

When you see it, say it. When someone does something well, you need to let them know right away. Don't store it up for later. If you wait, you will forget the specifics, and the employee will likely forget what happened. Hold yourself accountable for catching people doing things right every day. Focus on pinpointed behaviours that have been agreed upon in your coaching sessions. We all know that when an employee makes a mistake, we notice immediately and often address it immediately. Do the same for doing things right but far more often.

Concentrate on the behaviour, not the person. Feedback is never personal by intention, but it's often received personally. The best way to begin is by stating the behaviour under observation and asking the employee what impact they think it had on the client interaction. This focuses on the behaviour and its impact, not the individual. At times, employees will go to the personal, but as a manager, you can clarify that this is a coaching session on the behaviour and its impact on the client. This model enables you to avoid sounding accusatory by using "I" and focusing on behaviours instead of assumed interpretations. If you start with, "You really messed up with the client," that's accusatory and a personal attack. Instead, you could say, "I noticed that there wasn't a referral with this client. Let's talk about the scripting." To accentuate the positive feedback, we should say, "I loved the way you…" rather than, "You did a good job at…." It's not always easy, but if you practice, you will get really good at it.

Be specific. When giving positive feedback, tell the person *exactly* what they did well. This means both words and actions. Employee behaviour is what they say and do. Look for specific behaviours. Don't use generalizations such as "good attitude," "team player," or "dedicated worker." I know we all have heard these before, and they do make us feel good, but do they help us get any better? Do we really know what we did that was exceptional? Will we be able to repeat the behaviour?

Those generalizations can be misunderstood and lead to encouraging the wrong behaviour. Paint a picture for the person of what you saw them do or heard them say. Ask them what impact this had. This is where the real learning occurs. When employees can relate to the impact the behaviour has on a client, they can relate to the behaviour's consequences. Consequences can be positive or negative, but there is always one to be discussed. A consequence of effectively asking for a referral might be getting a name of a potential client. That's a positive consequence of a specific behaviour. As a coach, you need to help your employees make a connection between behaviour and consequences.

A good example of pointing out and reinforcing this connection would be, "I like the way you asked the client for the name of a family member or a friend that they could refer to you. You got two." Acknowledge the positive result and repeat the actual words the employee used to achieve it. Feedback has a powerful impact on repeating specific behaviour. Over time, the behaviour will become habit and improve performance.

Give more positives than negatives. For positive feedback to be heard and remembered, you must give it much more frequently than constructive feedback. A ratio that seems to be most effective is four positives to every constructive. I've interviewed many managers who tell me they give a lot of feedback, but their employees complain that they get little or none. Most of us have a tendency to remember bad news more than good news. Constructive feedback sticks with us longer and often hurts our feelings. It bursts our balloon of competence, and we often blame the manager for being insensitive. Since people will remember constructive feedback more than positive feedback, it's important to give the latter more than the former. The goal is to build on strengths, and the employee must realize that this is your intent. The best way to ensure employees find coaching worthwhile is to have this four-to-one balance in feedback. I know it's not easy to deliver this ratio, as we tend to find things wrong so we can help the employee get better.

Toastmasters International is a club designed to help people become better public speakers and communicators. After each speech, a designated person is the evaluator. The evaluator is instructed to provide four positive comments as feedback and one constructive comment. Toastmasters knows that if you want to change behaviour and performance, you need to build on strengths and build the confidence of the club members after their speeches. It works to develop speakers, and it works to develop employees too.

Focus on face-to-face feedback. Many managers feel they need to reward employees with gifts, awards, or prizes to recognize performance. In reality, most employees just want the boss to tell them face to face. There is power in a well-delivered piece of feedback when the boss looks an employee right in the eye and tells them exactly what they've done well. We all feel a sense of pride and accomplishment when this happens. Employees will appreciate the boss much more too.

I know you're busy, but don't fall into the trap of providing feedback through email. It's nice, but it has minimal impact. If you can't provide the feedback face to face, write a short personal note to the employee, outlining how pleased you are and exactly what they did. Take a look at the memorabilia you have saved up in your career. I bet you have two or three handwritten letters from some executive who complimented you on a job well done. Why did you save those and not their email counterparts? The reason is simple. Handwritten notes have far more impact because they are more personal. Don't forget this when dealing with your team.

Use staff meetings. Providing positive feedback in a public forum such as a meeting or power huddle has quite an impact on the receiver. It also highlights the right behaviour to the whole team. I have also found it useful to ask others on the team for a "shout out" to one of their peers at a meeting. In this case, it's one employee delivering feedback on something that another employee did well.

Sometimes as manager you may have to help them discover the specific behaviour and the impact, but it's an effective strategy. It can go a long way to enhancing peer-to-peer relationships and the entire working environment.

Don't assume. One of my managers early in my career explained the meaning of *assume*. He said that when you *assume* something, you are "making an ass of you and me." What this simply means is don't assume anything. I learned my lesson a few times when I made assumptions that were unfounded—and paid a price.

Quite often, managers assume that employees are receiving feedback the way it was intended simply because they're giving it on a regular basis. Many managers believe they are providing feedback and coaching, while employees often say they receive none. A simple solution to the problem of making assumptions is to tell employees when you are coaching and providing feedback. Communicate your intentions directly to avoid confusion or misunderstanding. Clarity is crucial in the feedback loop.

Practice management by walking around (MBWA). The only way to provide instant feedback is by walking around, observing your employees in action, and taking the time to comment. This is informal feedback, but it's quite effective and should be a part of your daily routine.

Recognition. In survey after survey, employees continue to indicate how important getting recognition for a job well done is to their overall job satisfaction. It even ranks far ahead of money as a motivator. Happy people are motivated people. Motivated people perform well and help grow your company. As a manager, you can increase profitability, service, productivity, teamwork, and all aspects of your business by implementing a coaching program with a well-defined feedback process. Start small and recognize someone today.

Constructive Feedback

Providing positive feedback is fun and rewarding to both the employee and the manager, but how do we deliver constructive feedback for poor performance? This is a challenge, but many of the same rules that we highlighted above still apply. Constructive feedback is not an attack on the person, nor is it designed to be negative by nature. Constructive feedback is designed to improve performance in a specific area.

If you are focusing on immediate constructive feedback, don't start the conversation with a positive comment. Hiding difficult news behind good news sets a dangerous precedent when you truly want to deliver positive feedback. Preceding bad news with good trains your people to expect the other shoe to drop. This, of course, hinders your ability to deliver good news later and hinders your ability to deal with the constructive feedback, as your employee will wait for the bad news to come. This approach doesn't engender trust, and it causes undue stress. Be open, honest, and specific with constructive feedback.

When delivering constructive feedback, allow the employee to present their own solutions to improve their behaviour. What will they do to improve? Get their commitment to do so. Your job then is to follow up and find them doing something right relative to the behaviour they need to develop.

Below are general guidelines for providing constructive feedback:

Speak sincerely. Don't downplay the importance of the feedback, but be polite and sincere in your comments about the behaviour. Remember, it's not personal, but the employee may respond personally, so be prepared to refocus on the behaviour if they do. As manager, you are setting the tone for the discussion, so keep it focused on what counts.

Maintain eye contact and use the words *you*, *me*, and *I*. Try to say things such as, "I've noticed that your results are well below target," or, "Your referrals are below expectation as you know already, so let's talk about the behaviours you're using to get referrals." Never talk about what others are saying or what the rumour mill has to say. Be specific about the performance gap, stick to the facts, and gain a commitment from the employee to improve the behaviour in question. Provide all feedback strictly on your own observations.

Ignore behaviour that should be ignored. Not everything that can be addressed should be. Focus on agreed-upon specific behaviours that yield results. Focusing on too many things yields minimal return for your time and confuses your people on what's really important. Let the little things go, and chase the big things.

Avoid extremes and absolutes. Stay away from words such as *always*, *never*, *most*, *least*, *severe*, *incredible*, *unconscionable*, *unacceptable*, *total*, *complete*, *utter*, *maddening*, *crippling*, *devastating*, *terrible*, *horrible*, *God-awful*, *crappy*, *deplorable*, and anything that ends in *-est*. Extreme words and absolutes lead to the employee taking it personally and becoming defensive immediately. When this happens, they no longer listen, as they are focused on defending themselves from personal attack. Besides, such language is often untrue and rude to the point of being obnoxious.

"I'm disappointed." These words have amazing power. On the rare occasion when I needed to reprimand my kids and provide constructive feedback, I would use these words. Use them sparingly, as they carry tremendous weight with everyone who cares about you. Your employees do care about you, and they care what you think of them as performers. However, in particularly important matters, if you really need to connect with an employee, try saying, "I'm disappointed with the way you...." Remember, you want to focus on the behaviour, not the person.

Anticipate resistance. Have you ever received tough feedback? How did you feel? Whenever you give constructive feedback, you don't need to guess what the employee is thinking; you've been there yourself, as have I. We are all a little hurt by these comments, and we may even get angry.

During a session of constructive feedback, ask the employee how they're feeling about it. Even if they say they're fine with it, they usually aren't. The most common response one spouse gives to another when asked if something is wrong is, "I'm fine." We usually know when the words don't match the tone. Allow time for employees to work through the emotions. Remember, we're not attacking the person but rather discussing their behaviour. The person is fine even if the behaviour isn't. Try to stick to only one issue at a time so you don't snow the employee under with a litany of problems.

Get a commitment. There is no point in just outlining the behaviour that needs attention without an effort to rectify it. Facilitate a discussion on how the employee can improve, and get to the specifics of the path to improvement. Document the revised behaviour and get their commitment to implement change. Don't waste your time and theirs by complaining about a problem and not helping resolve it. Turn the problem into an opportunity to boost performance.

Follow up. If the issue is important enough to have a meeting with the employee, it's important enough to follow up on the behaviour. Find an opportunity to see the employee doing something right or making progress. Be sure to take the time to point it out to them when it happens.

Management expert Ken Blanchard calls feedback the breakfast of champions. I agree completely because it's through feedback that we all learn and grow on our path to greatness. You should be asking your boss to provide feedback to you on your coaching skills.

This is how you develop these important skills. Ask your employees for feedback after you have delivered a coaching session. Their feedback will also be critical to your personal growth.

Make the commitment to use coaching and feedback as the best way to improve the performance of your team. Make a commitment to coach on a regular basis. Make a commitment to search out the bright spots in your company and discover people doing things right on a daily basis.

If I were to interview your employees and ask them about the feedback you give them, what would they say about it? There may be a thousand ways to do something wrong, but there are only a few ways to do it right. Learning from mistakes is admirable, but it would take a long time to eliminate all the wrong ways of doing something. It might take only one action to identify the right way.

Feedback really is all about catching someone doing something almost right. Catch your employees on the road to success and reward them for moving in the right direction. Recognize and celebrate them. It's like when a child learns to ride a bike for the first time. Parent cheer and celebrate each small improvement in balancing the bike towards stability. Few parents will set their child on a bike and make no comments until the child is a proficient rider. Most will encourage each step towards the eventual goal rather than wait until goal is achieved. Small short-term goals lead to continual encouragement, which leads to mastery over time. This works for every employee and every coach, and feedback is an essential part of the process.

Best Practices

1. Use positive feedback to reinforce behaviour.

2. Use constructive feedback to change behaviour.

3. Keep to a ratio of four positives to one constructive.

4. Remember that feedback is a benefit to employees, not a penalty.

5. Provide positive feedback immediately and in public.

6. Keep constructive feedback private.

7. Tell employees you are providing feedback so that they know they are being coached.

8. Ensure employees know that the feedback is professional, not personal.

9. Focus on the behaviour, not the person.

10. Focus on the key pinpointed behaviours.

Chapter 18
Coaching to Achieve Business Results

By Connie Bird

Coaching motivates performers to reach higher levels, to seek out opportunities, new skills, and new possibilities that help build momentum and increase results. This chapter will expand on the practices and values of effective coaching.

Trust and confidentiality are important aspects in the coaching relationship. Growth happens when people see a new possibility. A new perspective or new path opens up in the discussion when you are open, honest, and vulnerable. It's not easy to lay it all on the line and be vulnerable with your coach, especially when that person is also your boss.

Employees are worried that their vulnerabilities will be held against them, especially at performance appraisal time. If the coach does, it sabotages the coaching relationship. It could prevent employees from being vulnerable with them ever again. This is often the reason why companies bring in external coaches.

Do You Have the Right Material?
The company wants to fast-forward business results and will often decide to adopt a coaching program to do so. However, not all

managers make good coaches. A manager's job is to get results through their people. Yet, when you look at where the majority of their time is spent, you'll likely see them spending time on procedures, reporting, processes, managing personnel problems, and justifying the data. In many companies, people are working at and beyond capacity. Something has got to give if we are to change a manager's mandate from keeper of the process to truly being an effective coach. Do you have to take something off your plate if you want you to further develop your coaching skills and execute a coaching strategy consistently? What can you do to set yourself up for success?

As a manager, you need to develop the desire to become a good coach. It takes the right attitude, skill development, and lots of practice. When a coaching program is deemed ineffective, it's often viewed as a program failure rather than a problem with the manager being underdeveloped as a coach. To sustain increases in results, the coaching program must be sustained through training, coaching skill refreshers, observations with feedback, and accountability. Successful coaches must develop themselves before they can lead their employees to their own development goals and increased results. It takes years for managers to develop as coaches, provided they have opportunities to practice as a coach and influence the behaviour of their employees.

If you want to get extraordinary results from your people, you need to develop yourself as an extraordinary coach. Invest in your own development. Be intentional about developing your coaching skills and processes. Ask for feedback from your boss, your employees, and your peers. It will help tremendously if your boss follows the coaching protocols established by your company and you're not in competition with your peers. You are in competition with the competition.

Alignment

Coaching is a perk, a privilege to those forward-thinking employees who are interested in an investment in their personal growth and increasing results. When an employee is open to coaching, the investment of time is much more lucrative, and any increased frequency of meaningful discussions helps hone or change behaviour.

When I was working on *Life Is Sales* with Gary, I hired a professional coach. I had a weekly thirty-minute call before the crack of dawn because coaching didn't fit into my normal workday as a sales professional and author. It was an incredible time in my life. I made powerful choices as to where I was investing my time so I could get the results I wanted. As a full-time sales professional and family woman, I never would have thought I would be a published author in three books. I had that can-do attitude, developed the skills, laid down a process that worked for me, practiced, got feedback, and moved further and further. There was a cost to being coached. There was a fee and an even more precious cost: the investment of my time. I was, however, open to being coached. I was authentic.

There is a difference to me between honesty and authenticity. We are honest with each other; being authentic is being honest with the person in the mirror. I was straight with my coach about my fears and about being overcommitted. He helped me make doable commitments each week. I felt accountable and I fully intended to honour my word. Most weeks I did, but some weeks I didn't. After the difficult weeks, I didn't want to go to the following week and say I didn't do what I said I would for the second week in a row. Keeping on track, I accomplished even more than I thought was possible in my life.

Being bigger than you know yourself to be is an incredible feeling. My coach held me to a high standard and helped me grow beyond what I thought I was capable of. I was truly stretched and felt really alive! I was living life to its fullest, but it wasn't easy, as I faced many challenges along the way. We celebrated small accomplishments and my desired outcome. I truly had a trusted partner vested in my success. I am proud of my expanded personal capacity and pleased to have achieved the result I set out to accomplish.

To Coach or to Train

One busy morning in my bank branch, I lent a hand on cash transactions. Having the manager at the counter was always good for a laugh from the staff and our customers. The teller beside me was struggling with her sales, so I watched her behaviour as I worked. I saw her problem. When the line died down, I told her what she should do. Instead of her just taking the customer's order in each moment, I told her that next time she should look at their portfolio of business with the bank.

"I can't do that," she said.

I replied, "Think of what the customer is missing and ask a couple of questions to uncover another of their needs and an opportunity for you to increase your sales."

She nodded, gave me a quick half-hearted smile, and barely made eye contact.

There, I thought, I've set her straight. Now she's on her way.

The next week, I checked her sales results—no change. What was her problem? I told her exactly what to do! Why wasn't she doing it?

The problem wasn't just her; it was also in my approach with her. At that time, branch managers would ask themselves, "Can the employee do what I'm asking if their life depended upon it?" If the answer was yes, our job was to counsel the employee. If the answer was no, then our job was to coach.

If the job was to coach, we got out the training manual and had the employee study it. We then paired them up with a peer to teach them how they do the job. We then had the peer observe the employee do it before sending them off to do the job they were hired to do. By today's standards, this is *not* coaching; this is teaching or training. We had it wrong back then, and perhaps some of us have it wrong today. Some managers wrongly believe it's their job to simply hire, train, and send employees off to do the job they were hired to do.

If the job was to counsel the employee, we would ask them what the problem was and then help solve it, often telling them what we would do if we were in their shoes. Sometimes it worked, and like the story above, many times it didn't.

After six to nine months of training, most employees are deemed competent enough to do their job. By that time, how many of us like being told what to do by our boss, or by anyone for that matter? When I'm competent, I really don't take too kindly to being told what to do. I get my back up a little. I often wonder what's wrong with the person who feels this sudden need to teach me something I already know. It takes some self-talk to reframe the situation before I see that this person is just trying to help me. They really aren't telling me that I'm a total idiot and don't know what I'm doing, so why do they need to *tell* me what to do? Managers want to help their employees be successful, but they make the mistake of teaching when really they should be coaching.

Our Roles As Managers

As managers develop as coaches, they begin to see their job as multifaceted. They get that they aren't supposed to solve employees' problems. They know it's better to have employees solve their own problems relative to their experience and values to get each employee's commitment to improve.

To make a point with the managers who continue to tell competent employees what to do, I say to them, "After providing your solution to the employee, add just two words to the end of your sentence: *you loser*." I rant, "Yes, because clearly the employee is incompetent, and you need to solve their problems for them." It gets a laugh, and the manager becomes more self-aware of their demeaning behaviour. A good coach asks the employee for solutions to the situation. We call this the gentle art of self-discovery. If the employee is stumped, and the problem isn't urgent, have them leave the coaching discussion to ponder a solution and come back. If the problem is urgent, the manager may offer up an idea.

Some managers are exasperated by how often their employees are coming to them for answers to their problems. Their email is overflowing and the phone is ringing. After months and years of solving other people's problems, it's hard to see how managers have caused this aberrant behaviour in their employees. It was they who enabled this dependency.

A colleague of mine shared that he was frustrated by his employees pulling him, and he was never getting to his own to-do list. He counted how many decisions he made—eighty-eight in just one day. No wonder he was exhausted. We discussed the different roles a manager plays with an employee. He saw the problem. He understood that if he wanted to change behaviour in his employees, he had to change his own behaviour first. This is easier said than done. We came up with a strategy that allowed him to help both himself and his employees.

Today, I see coaching in a very different light from the old definition of coaching or counselling. As managers, we have different roles to play in getting our team to achieve business goals:

1. If an employee is unable to do what we want them to do, we teach or train.
2. We need to set direction, conveying why we are doing so, setting clear expectations for performance, getting an agreement, and checking to ensure the employee understands.
3. We problem solve with the employee, getting rid of obstacles so they can do what we ask them to do.
4. After the above points are covered, we are left to coach and motivate.

What Is Coaching?

Effective coaching is not teaching, setting expectations, or problem solving. Coaching is the art of asking thoughtful questions and generously listening so employees can discover for themselves what there is to do more of or differently to achieve better results. These thoughtful questions are at the core of coaching. A good coach lets go of personal agendas and supports employees in their development. A coach celebrates successes and supports employees in solving their own problems through their own unique answers.

A good coach facilitates the coaching discussion with employees. Given time, employees will discover their own answers—new ways of being based on their values, preferences, experiences, and unique perspectives. Our answers to their challenges are not their answers. Employees are much more likely to execute their own ideas than they are to comply with suggestions from their boss. We want employees to feel empowered and inspired to act when coaching discussions end.

Teach, Observe, Feedback

Some organizations invest in teaching leadership and management skills but miss out on supporting the manager once the lessons are over. We know learners only take in a small portion of what is taught in the classroom. Many managers struggle with applying these lessons to their own personal work environment. Continued support is required if the transference of these skills is to occur. Observational coaching and a community forum of like learners assist in keeping the lessons alive.

As human beings, we are meaning-making machines. We see and hear something and cannot help but automatically judge and put our own labels on what happened. As a manager, you gain credibility by observing agreed-upon pinpointed behaviours. Document what employees say and do so it can be discussed. Avoid your interpretations of the event, but stick with the behaviour observed as fact.

Observe employees in action, discuss strengths and opportunities, and provide feedback on the application of agreed-upon behaviours. I recommend the "ask then tell" approach to providing observational feedback. What employees thinks of themselves is more important than what we think of them. Ask first, and then provide your insights. Quote specifically what employees say or do, as it brings value to the conversation and supports your opinions.

The pitfall of observational feedback is getting sucked in too deep into the customer interaction. Your goal is to observe the employee, not the customer. Sometimes we want to solve the customer's situation for the employee, but this defeats the purpose of the exercise. Your focus should remain on the employee. The closer you get to those who influence the customer to deal with your company, the faster you will move towards improved results.

When I observe a coach in action with an employee, I ask for some information, such as: How long has the employee been on the job? What did the employee agree to do in the last coaching session? What positive feedback are you prepared to offer the employee? In many observations, the manager launches into a teaching session. Is this the correct role to play in a coaching session? The answer is often, "Well, the employee promised to do it and never did—twice now—so I thought I'd better teach them how." When you feel the urge to teach (as I often do in this situation), this is the time to ask yourself, "Could the employee do it if their life depended upon it?" Yes means that coaching is the best solution. If the answer is no, schedule another session of training or have the employee explore other resources to fill gaps in knowledge or skills.

Aligning the Management Team
We have so many priorities at work, so many goals to achieve. The boss gives us eight or ten objectives to achieve throughout the year. Inevitably, two or three new ones are added to the list. With too many things to focus on, we lose all focus and get stuck.

I recommend coaching to achieve one or two business results that require your employees to change their behaviour. In your coaching discussions, determine specific behaviours employees need to carry out to effectively achieve desired outcomes. All the competing priorities will hang around, but they will no longer monopolize your coaching time. What you focus on gets done. Resist coaching a variety of behaviours. Start with the result you want, and then determine what behaviours will get you there. These behaviours should become the focus for coaching.

You, your employees, and your managers up the ladder must all focus on the same one or two business priorities and maintain that focus. You need to resist changing the focus week after week, or even month after month. The communication of this focus must remain consistent from all levels to maintain employee focus. If they are constantly reminded of the most important objective deserving focused attention, they will focus on it. Leaders have to walk the talk. Employees are watching and listening.

The goal is to change behaviour to achieve results. It will take time. We want pinpointed behaviours to become good habits. It takes time to form the habits necessary to achieve the result we want. Once a behaviour becomes an ingrained habit, we can stop coaching it and focus on something else. If results slip, we need to check our assumption that the behaviour was an ingrained habit. Only when a behaviour is self-sustaining should you feel comfortable with moving on to new objectives in the coaching process.

Pinpointed Behaviour

Consider what the star performers do and pinpoint the exact behaviour for all on the team to replicate. Behaviour goes beyond mere activities. Pinpointed behaviour is looking specifically for what the employee says and does to get the desired outcome.

We need to then set out the direction to all our performers as to what the expectation is and how we will measure what success looks like. Our goal is to get the performers doing the pinpointed behaviour with the consistency and with quality to achieve the business goal. To change behaviour in others, we often have to start by pointing the finger at ourselves and changing our behaviour first. Consistency is so important for coaching to be effective. Do not cancel coaching sessions! If something more important has come up, reschedule your appointment.

Keep Focused

As a passionate sales professional and a coach to sales coaches, one of my weaknesses is losing my coaching focus. I occasionally get so absorbed in the employee's sales interaction with the customer that I lose focus on the manager I'm observing. Knowing this about myself, I give my clients permission to bring me back on track to discussing them. Some clients see my separate skills sets as a strength and will contract with me to do both: a brief three-minute discussion about the employee's sales behaviours and then the real discussion focused on the manager's application of their skills.

Even though I coach as a profession, I can still get off track, so I do understand how difficult it is to keep focused on the actual coaching and observations. Just keep at it, and you will get the results you're looking for.

Best Practices

1. Learn how to foster trust and openness in your coaching sessions.

2. Develop yourself as a coach, not just a manager.

3. Make a personal commitment to be a great coach.

4. Ask for coaching feedback from your boss, peers, and employees.

5. Know the difference between training and coaching.

6. Coaching is about the employee, not the customer—and focus on the behaviour, not the individual.

7. Be fair but firm in your assessment and dialogue.

8. Get everyone on board on every level as you focus on one or two priorities at a time.

9. Be consistent in your coaching, and make coaching appointments.

10. Keep focused.

Chapter 19
Time Management/ Change Management

In my research, I have found that most managers name time management and change management as the two most difficult parts of their job. When asked what limits their ability to achieve their goals, they almost universally say they don't have enough time. Dealing with change and continually shifting priorities make managing time a real challenge. Rather than coaching behaviours for better results, managers are constantly dealing with the current activities of their changing work environment. This chapter provides simple solutions that will free up more of your time and energy to focus on developing people. This is what makes the difference in most companies.

Time management has been an employee issue for decades, and I expect it will be a serious issue for decades to come. Communication has become a primary focus for all organizations. We all go off to training sessions to learn how to be better communicators and listeners, and yet our challenges with time continue and are even exacerbated by new technologies that are supposed to help. Doing more with less allows a company to decrease costs while increasing business. How we handle the demands of the job and the demands of being "in communication" will help determine our proficiency with time management.

We cannot actually *manage* time; we can only manage what we do in the time we allocate. There are sixty seconds in every minute and sixty minutes in every hour. In my seminars, I ask who among the attendees are good at time management. I ask those who say they're good at it to demonstrate how they manage time. We can't manage the clock; it just keeps on ticking at exactly the same pace day in and day out. Time is the constant, while our activities are the variable. We can only manage the variable. It's what we do in the time available that is the true measure of our ability to manage ourselves within time.

Time Wasters

One of the most effective ways to free up time to do what matters is to eliminate the activities that are essentially wasteful of this precious commodity. Below are the most common time wasters that affect all of us along with tips for reeling in the activities associated with them:

Email. The number one culprit is email. Our demands for more and more information mean we are all inundated with email. The problem lies in how many we get, how many we deal with, and how we deal with them. We tend to drop whatever we're doing to respond to an email when our smartphone vibrates or our computer beeps to inform us of an all-important email. Effective email management can save you four to five hours a week. Here are some suggestions to gain control over your email:

1. Turn off your email four times a day for an hour at a time and focus your energy on the task at hand. Don't be interrupted. It takes as much as three minutes or more to get back to the task every time the email beeps for your attention.
2. Turn your email on for ten to fifteen minutes every couple of hours, and deal with the items immediately. You should deal with no more than ten inbox items at a time. Scrolling through

email alone burns two hours a week.

3. Unless absolutely necessary, never reply if you are only carbon copied (cc'd) in an email or use "reply all." You may become part of the problem.

4. Your emails should be a maximum of one page (i.e., one screen). If what you're trying to say will take more than that, phone the person or visit them and resolve the issue immediately.

5. Use your phone or face-to-face communication for important decision-making issues rather than delay everything through massive email responses.

6. Use the delete button often. If it's really important, you will get a second email—often when it's not important too.

7. Use priority codes for time-sensitive issues.

8. Use the search feature to find items that need attention.

Meetings. These are the second-largest time waster. The problem stems from the common belief that meetings are a reflection of communication, productivity, and getting things done. However, many meetings are useless and need not happen in the first place. Here are suggestions for holding meetings that count and avoiding ones that don't:

1. Never go to meetings unless you're going to speak, otherwise it's an update meeting and you don't need a meeting to be updated.

2. If you're holding a meeting, ask yourself the following questions beforehand: What is the one thing I want people to know? How do I want people to feel? What do I want people to do as a result of the meeting?

3. We all attend meetings we find useless—don't go anymore.

4. Meetings should be one hour maximum and must start on time.

5. Limit attendance to those who can talk about the meeting's focus.

6. Have an agenda, and include a pre-read where appropriate, sent to attendees two days prior to the meeting.
7. Make a decision to avoid having to follow up with another meeting.
8. Try a meeting with no chairs and see how quickly it will be over.
9. Cut your number of meetings in half immediately.
10. Focus on seeing more customers rather than meeting with employees.

Having too many priorities. Priorities are the items of utmost importance. Having priorities doesn't work, however, if you try to focus on too many at a time. If you have ten priorities, you don't have any. Below is some advice on how to focus on what's essential:

1. Set your priorities and don't be a victim—choose what to do.
2. Repeat the priorities to your team often; they forget.
3. Keep to three or four priorities maximum—one or two is even better.
4. You should only have one short-term priority at a time.
5. Priorities help everyone decide what to say yes to and what to say no to.
6. Choose tasks that correlate directly with your priorities.
7. Just say no. To-do items run downhill in an organization. Learn to manage your boss and reduce your stress and workload to achieve your priorities.
8. Learn how to say no while maintaining relationships.
9. Ask why five times before accepting a new priority.

Procrastination. This is the time management killer in all of us. Sometimes getting started is the difficult thing. Sometimes finishing a task becomes a challenge. Below are tips for avoiding avoidance and getting things done one step at a time:

1. Set daily objectives that focus on your priorities.
2. Keep your objectives small, but keep them visible.
3. Share objectives with others—this helps you focus on them.
4. Learn to manage your negative self-talk. Fear of failure and rejection feeds procrastination. Keep positive.
5. Keep lists and strike out each task as you accomplish them. It's very rewarding.
6. Just do it. Once you get started, you may find a task is easier than you thought it would be.
7. When in a rut, repeat to yourself, "If it's to be, it's up to me."

What to Do

You now have many tips on eliminating time wasters. Now it's up to you to decide what you will do next. This requires you to change your habits, and it's not easy. Choose something simple such as turning off your email for three or four hours every day at intervals, and see if you notice anything. I guarantee you will be more focused on your projects and your job for longer periods. Do this Monday morning, and by the end of the week, you will have accomplished more than you thought possible. Small wins in time management will lead to more control over what you do and when you do it.

You have no reason to keep complaining about your workload when you are probably wasting easily four to five hours a week on time wasters. What will you do with those extra hours you reclaim? What can you accomplish with this extra time each week? The choice is yours.

Change Management

The next largest challenge is dealing with change. As a manager, you are nothing short of the implementer of change. You are the one who executes changes within your team. If there is one constant in management, it's that things will change and change often. Just look at the technological changes of the past ten years. We can hardly imagine what the future holds. Ten years ago, the iPod was just beginning to revolutionize the music industry and Bluetooth technology was just getting a foothold in the market. There was no iPhone or iPad, and Bluetooth-enabled devices weren't as ubiquitous as they are today. Now we carry powerful computers in our pockets, the Internet is available to us virtually everywhere we go, software has exploded onto the marketplace, and the work we do has changed dramatically. The Information Age has truly arrived. Are we ready?

Every company leader wants change to happen. They want their managers to be change agents. So how best to implement change and gain the commitment of the staff to deliver on a consistent basis?

The Buy-In

The term *buy-in* is a misnomer that will lead change agents down the wrong path. Gaining a commitment to change is not a sales game. Don't "sell" change to people as a way of accelerating agreement and implementation. Selling change to people is not a sustainable strategy for success, as it will come back to bite you at the least opportune time. When people listen to a leader selling them on a change, the good employees will usually smile and give the appearance of agreement, but they are likely thinking, "Another head office debacle coming our way, but if I wait, it will pass like all the others." The more conservative types chat amongst themselves, saying, "This will never work. Why do they keep wanting to change when we're already successful?" They may even actively sabotage the change effort.

Change needs to be understood in terms that make sense to people. For anything to change, people have to start behaving differently. This is the key to managing a successful change. If you focus on behaviour, you will see results. To change behaviour, the change must appeal to people's logical minds and to their emotions. It seems we have two systems at work inside our brain: the planner and the doer.

In their book *Switch: How to Change Things When Change Is Hard*, Chip Heath and Dan Heath talk about the rider and the elephant. The rider is the logical side while the elephant is the emotional side of all of us, and the two compete for control. We can convince the rider to change through logic, but the analytical mind will always want more detail and will procrastinate. The doer is the elephant, and it needs to be motivated to move forward. Since the two compete in different ways within the mind of employees—the planner side and the doer side—nothing changes unless we as managers appeal to both the rider and the elephant.

According to the Heath brothers, "Big problems are rarely solved with commensurately big solutions. Instead, they are most often solved by a sequence of small solutions, sometimes over weeks and sometimes over decades." By focusing on small solutions, we as managers can work towards solving big problems through the work of our employees. The focus of change management, therefore, should not be on the big problem we face, but rather the essential solutions that together move things towards the ultimate goal.

Bright Spots

In assessing the need for change, we usually look for all the things that are wrong. These things are usually easy to spot because we have problems such as declining sales, poor service, or high turnover. These are serious issues, and so we look at all the things we're doing wrong to come up with a thorough complex plan of change to address our "gaps."

If we change our perspective for a moment and decide to look at what's working and how we can do more of that, our options change. In every problem there are always people or processes that are outperforming. We should look at these and determine what it is they're doing and then replicate that. This is what the Heath brothers call "finding the bright spots."

We tend to look for performance gaps and focus our change

management on what's wrong. When your twelve-year-old comes home with a report card that has two As, two Bs, one C, and one F, where do your thoughts and words go immediately? You can't help yourself: You immediately focus on the F and try to work out a strategy to improve it. You focus on what's wrong and consider solutions such as hiring a tutor and banning video games for a month until the grade improves.

Using our coaching process of building on strengths, we might instead say, "Wow! You got two As. Congratulations. What is it about these courses that help you do so well, and how can you use these strengths to work on the F?" This is a simple shift from what's wrong to a "the bright spot" that a student can build on.

This same propensity to focus on the negative occurs in your management role all the time when you should instead focus on what's going well to see how it can work in other areas. Let's see how we can apply this to change management.

Make It Small

Change is hard enough even when the end goal is clear. To appeal to both the logical mind and our emotional side, look at the change and break it down into simple small steps that are easily understood and implemented. In accomplishing each step, people feel good about their contribution and everyone moves forward. The challenge we all face is that we expect everyone to see the big picture and to understand each step without clarification. To avoid confusion, actually script out the small steps needed to accomplish the change. Be absolutely clear in your directions. Be specific. In sales, we often script the actual words that will be used until everyone becomes comfortable with the process, and then it becomes a matter of each salesperson's own style.

To improve their customer service image, Tim Hortons started to have the drive-through operators introduce themselves over the intercom. Now why would this be important? And if service was an issue at Tim Hortons, why did they start there? They have fresh competition from McDonald's and Starbucks, and their service experience was declining. I imagine the head office spent countless hours looking at what everyone was doing wrong and presenting wholesale changes to improve service.

What they actually did was start small with a specific change: Have the staff introduce themselves to clients. This is an easy change and can be monitored constantly if necessary. I have noticed that they're now consistent in this approach, but in the beginning, it didn't happen every time. Once this is perfect and becomes a "bright spot," they can move on to the next simple phase. They believe that if the drive-through operators introduce themselves, it will create a different and more personal experience for their customers, and happier customers like the coffee better. If Tim Hortons' stock price is any indication, the approach is working well.

Motivate to Begin

In most companies today, leadership focuses on strategy, culture, systems, or internal structure. They rarely look at the most important aspect of change, which is changing the behaviour of people. As with the theory of the rider and elephant, change in people's behaviour is usually achieved by engaging their feelings.

The reason why small changes work in delivering big change is because we all become engaged emotionally when something works and we are successful. Success builds success, and positive reinforcement is the best way to move change initiatives forward. The smaller the change, the easier it will be to find people doing something right, and we build from there.

With each small win, people feel less nervous about change; they feel less reluctant to move forward because they get a taste of success. Change is a journey, not an event that can be dictated. Have a look back in your own business life to see what changes worked and what ones didn't. Have a closer look at those that worked, and you will find the bright spots that will help you next time.

Trust

Trust is the cornerstone to any change initiative. If employees trust their manager or the company leadership, this will make the change that much easier. If there is a lack of trust, we run into a brick wall. As a manager, you will smooth any change initiative by maintaining trust with your employees and constantly validating your trustworthiness.

You cannot impose change—people and teams need to be empowered to find their own solutions and responses, with facilitation and support from managers and tolerance and compassion from leaders and executives. Management and leadership style and staff behaviours are more important than clever processes and overwrought policies. Employees need to be able to trust the organization and its leaders. Trust infuses change initiatives with credibility.

If you lose the trust of your employees, it won't matter what the leaders say. It will always be taken with a grain of salt. Any change initiatives in an environment devoid of trust will be suspect. Employees will constantly watch out for ulterior motives, and the company will face an uphill battle. When delivering change, have your trustworthy leader deliver the message. It's up to you as a trustworthy manager to manage the process.

Change causes an emotional response in most people, managers included. Our first reaction to change is usually one of disbelief (just another flavour of the month), rejection (this won't really happen), or denial (this won't happen to me). Next, as the change progresses through the company, many people will shift to anger or resistance to the change. Certain people may actually attempt to sabotage the change. Fear and a lack of motivation are also potential problems.

As the change progresses, people begin to realize that it's inevitable and slowly start to accept it. They will begin to explore the means to accommodate the change and become creative in finding solutions to make it work. Finally, they become motivated by the challenges as they reconcile their former positions on the change and make a commitment to deliver.

Most of us go through these stages. When we realize this as a manager, it allows us to coach our employees through the stages quickly and smoothly rather than reject our employees' responses as unacceptable. When dealing with people, we must also deal with their emotions. When we know how they're feeling, we have a more proactive way of coaching them through the changes and help them find success.

Making Assumptions

There is a story you can find floating around the Internet that presents itself as a radio transcript of an actual conversation between a U.S. naval ship and a Canadian maritime contact off the coast of New-foundland in October 1995. The tale, in various versions featuring different nationalities, has circulated widely in emails, books, and websites for many years, and it has been used by numerous speakers and writers to illustrate lessons related to negotiation, making assumptions, and other themes. Unfortunately, the story isn't true; it never happened. Nevertheless, it's a great one. If you choose to use this as a teaching analogy, you will probably be forgiven for not revealing the truth of its validity until after telling the story.

Americans: "Please divert your course 15 degrees north to avoid a collision."

Canadians: "Recommend you divert YOUR course 15 degrees south to avoid collision."

Americans: "This is the captain of a U.S. Navy ship; I say again divert YOUR course."

Canadians: "No, I say again, you divert YOUR course."

Americans: "THIS IS THE AIRCRAFT CARRIER USS LIN-
COLN, THE SECOND LARGEST SHIP IN THE
UNITED STATES' ATLANTIC FLEET. WE ARE
ACCOMPANIED BY THREE DESTROYERS,
THREE CRUISERS, AND NUMEROUS SUP-
PORT VESSELS. I DEMAND THAT YOU
CHANGE YOUR COURSE 15 DEGREES
NORTH—THAT'S ONE-FIVE DEGREES
NORTH—OR COUNTERMEASURES WILL BE
UNDERTAKEN TO ENSURE THE SAFETY OF
THIS SHIP."

Canadians: "This is a lighthouse Your call."

This story is a funny yet valuable lesson in making wrong assumptions, especially where an obstacle is misinterpreted to be movable
when, in fact, it's not. The lesson, of course, is that making assumptions on something based on incomplete information can be disas-
trous. As a manager, you need to ensure your employees are
comfortable with keeping communication open with you, rather
than having them make wrong assumptions about what's going on.
An open-door policy and regular management by walking around
(MBWA) are ways to avoid having this happen. Of course, it's important that you don't make assumptions either, whether it's about
your team or your own bosses.

Change management is a hot topic with countless great books
and even more consultants offering the magic bullet to your change
woes. One of the best books on change I have read is *Switch: How
to Change Things When Change Is Hard* by Chip Heath and Dan
Heath. It provides a unique perspective on human nature and how
to capitalize on delivering sustainable change.

We all generally resist change to a degree. The usual reason is
because we don't understand why or what to do. We all need to be
reminded on a regular basis of the whys and the whats. Confusion

is the largest enemy of any change initiative. That's why clarification is critical and why making the steps small is the steady and sure way to reach the goal.

Be patient and win the long-term battles.

Best Practices

1. Scale down the amount of time you spend on time wasters: email, meetings, having too many priorities, and procrastination.

2. Don't try to sell a change by trying to get a buy-in from employees—help employees understand what the change means.

3. Solve big problems through small solutions.

4. Focus on the bright spots when bridging gaps.

5. Keep the steps towards change small and achievable—success builds on success.

6. Keep the steps clear and specific, as it helps employees become comfortable while working towards change.

7. Maintain trust with your employees and they will be more open to change.

8. Keep in mind your employees' logical and emotional responses to change and help them manage each type.

9. Don't make assumptions—keep communication between you and your employees open and accessible.

Chapter 20

Remote Management: Managing What You Can't See

By Gary Laughlin
President, GHL & Associates Ltd.

I first started remotely managing a sales force over twenty years ago. They were on 100 percent commission and worked from home. Up until then, I had always managed a group of people in an office, where every work-related conversation was across the table face to face. I could see what people were doing every day—who they were talking to, and even what they were saying. I could see everything that was going on within the branch. As the manager, my favourite tools were command and control, and I had the ultimate responsibility for the monthly results of the group.

Shifting to manage a group from a distance was very intimidating. Managing people you can't see was new to many people in the financial services industry. We didn't have any manuals and had very little in the way of employee guidelines or HR policies. We had little, if any, training, so in many ways, we found ourselves making up policy as we went along. We tried to interpret existing guidelines and made them fit for a sales group that interacted with clients outside of a traditional bricks-and-mortar environment.

The Artful Dodger

When you remotely manage a team of people in any business, you quickly realize just how different everyone is and how they approach and view issues differently. In the early days of having weekly individual telephone conversations with my team, it became very apparent that not everyone saw the value in these discussions as much as I did. I had one individual who I referred to as "the Artful Dodger." He had the great misfortune of missing so many calls that his behaviour became obvious to me. His territory was very large, and in those days, cell phone coverage was spotty in rural markets. It did prove challenging if you were between cell towers.

Many of our phone calls were scheduled at the same day and same time every week, but he always found himself on the road between here and wherever. He was either getting called away unexpectedly or experiencing problems driving that caused him to be in the wrong place to either take or make a call. It was unfortunate because I was always on the phone or with others in between calls when he called me back, and we really didn't have the quality of discussions we both wanted. I felt so bad for him for the longest time. Here he was struggling to make his targets and not receiving any support from his manager. *Poor him.*

Now, in reality, it didn't take long for me to catch onto what I would describe, at best, as avoidance, and I was really starting to enjoy the weekly excuses and actually looked forward to what he was going to come up with next. He had an endless supply, and I found it difficult not to laugh.

I can't imagine the energy he wasted in avoiding me and what would have happened if he applied this same energy to his job. This level of creativity would have enhanced his performance and put money in his pocket. After a while, it was necessary to bring the ruse to an end and get on with the business at hand. Our HR policy dictated that I was required to issue a warning and put the Artful Dodger on notice. So armed with several months of telephone bills (which the company paid for) and our call diary, he and I were quickly able to determine that he was not on the road as much as he thought, and on those specific call dates, his car never left the driveway.

The moral of the story is that even the Artful Dodger can be managed remotely. Once his game was exposed, he admitted that this was not the job for him, and we parted company. I often wonder how long he would have remained with the company if I hadn't addressed his behaviour.

Have a Partner

I had a colleague living and working in Alberta who was also managing remotely. We talked often about how to mitigate some of the risk while still trying to conform to company policy that reflects a branch working environment. Our challenge was to apply common-sense principles while making things up as we went along, all the while hoping we wouldn't get fired. We both were experiencing the same issues, and it was important for both of us to know that we weren't alone. Our bosses were having some difficulty with the logistics of managing an external sales force too and basically left it up to us to determine how to proceed. If you can find a partner to share and discuss approaches, it helps keep you on track and motivated.

Organizationally, many industries and companies have come a long way since those early days. It would seem that companies with large sales groups have had a slight lead in developing policies and procedures that allow for more people to work remotely, while smaller companies are looking for ways to make it work for them and their employees. The upside of remote management far outweighs what is perceived as risk. I'll get into this more in a moment.

Even today, the very thought of being responsible for the achievement of goals and results of others remains a very serious concern for many people, especially when they can't see what others are doing every day. It's a great test of a manager's skill. The remote manager must develop new and different skills and, perhaps more important, other senses. The reliance on sight is replaced with hearing and listening.

Technology

People tend to credit the advancement of technology for the migration to remote management. Technology today has had a significant impact on just about every aspect of our lives and business, but the actual management of the people hasn't changed that much. Management is still concerned with personal one-on-one coaching. Unless you're using NASA satellites, you still can't see what your people are doing every day, let alone know where they are, who they're talking to, what they're saying, or, of course, what the customer is doing. This leads us to the question: Did you ever need to know these things to that extent? As much as technology has enhanced so many aspects of our lives and business, it still hasn't replaced the need for quality conversations.

Where it has had a huge impact is in the way we can now communicate on a personal level for business. Various sales-reporting software programs allow managers to monitor activity and compare it to results. Each sales visit includes commentary from the salesperson on what happened, which is a valuable tool for follow-ups. Managers can access these software programs and verify the quality of the notes, the meetings, and the results. Programs such as Salesforce provide excellent monitoring tools, but they still don't replace the need for personal observation.

The impact developing technologies have had on business communication is significant. We have come a long way in a very short period. Cell phones are no longer the size of bricks. Fax machines now belong in museums next to rotary telephones. Everything is in real time now, and instant means within a nanosecond. We have gone from having a meeting to having my smartphone connect to your computer. We now have an abundance of communication options—so many, in fact, that it can be a challenge to get around to having an actual quality voice-to-voice conversation.

The goal is to avoid letting technology become the answer. Instead, let it be the means to allow us to have more meaningful discussions. It's not just the method of communicating that's important; it's also the content and context. With less dialogue going on between people, it's more important now than ever to make sure your discussions are meaningful, purposeful, and in line with your desired outcomes. Communicating garbage with the best, most cutting-edge equipment in the world still produces garbage. I see this happen when friends get a new smartphone. I get bombarded with whatever new feature the phone has. After a while, or at least until the next release, it fades away.

Tools can quickly become toys. Make sure you use them with purpose.

Communication

Although technology is important, it's not everything. Communication is the critical component in managing a remote sales force, but it needs to be meaningful and purposeful. Managing remotely has a significant upside for business, but it's an initiative that isn't without its risks. There are inherent risks in every business initiative, whether large or small. There is also the risk of doing nothing or going too fast or too slow. Mitigating risks in implementation and execution of a new initiative will help determine the outcome. The largest risk, of course, is that your salespeople are staying home like our "Artful Dodger," or your employees are just not performing, and it takes too long to notice and take action.

There is now a vast selection of books about managing a remote workforce, and you can also find material on the Internet or attend any of the myriad training sessions now available. For the most part, they all share some common elements and come to the same conclusion: You get out of it what you put into it.

What I have learned through an awful lot of trial and error is that you can effectively expand your remote management capability by having predetermined and agreed-upon goals and objectives for both activities and results supported by regular communication routines. Having a weekly telephone conversation about the outcomes of last week's activities and establishing new objectives for the week ahead is more than enough content to ensure meaningful and purposeful discussions. It's helpful to discuss weekly activities that focus on achieving the results that you discuss monthly.

As a manager, your challenge during these calls is in being consistent and staying focused on each individual's activities and results as compared to their commitments. It's easy to drift off topic or move from specifics to a general conversation. It's the difference between discussing "need to do" versus "nice to do." In my own experience, I found that I was often facilitating rather than directing the dialogue. A remote sales force requires constant reminders of what's important and what the precise focus is. Since they don't see a boss every day, they are more easily sidetracked by peers, customers, or their own activities. The weekly call refocuses them on what is critical to their success. Consistency is the critical element to a successful remote workforce.

As a manager transitioning from a traditional structure to a remote structure, you will have many learning experiences. Given how long ago I started, I have probably learned more than most and without the benefit of reading it in a book. You will quickly learn what works and what doesn't.

Management Is a Discipline

Remote management is definitely not for everyone. As a manager, you have to realize that not everyone on your team hears and sees things the same way you do, nor do they all accept change the same way at the same time. Take the time to read the change management and coaching material in this book.

From an employee perspective, moving from a group environment in an office to working from home requires a different level of discipline and self-management. I used to see the impact it had on new hires. For as long as they worked, they talked about wanting to be self-employed and self-reliant. They would claim they would accomplish so much more if only they could work from home and choose their most productive hours. Be careful what you wish for. After a year at home, most found it difficult to remain focused all day. They discovered they were less effective in a housecoat than if they got dressed. They also discovered two or three days at home alone was tough; they needed more human contact.

This is where goals and a communication routine really have an impact. When I reflect back, I can think of a few learning curves that I wish I had avoided, and there are a few that I still laugh at to this day. I also learned that not everyone likes communication routines.

Goals

I learned long ago that the secret to managing people isn't just communicating effectively; it's also the way goals and objectives were determined to begin with. The investment of time upfront in determining goals and objectives for both activities and results will be the biggest determining factor in the achievement of the individual's, the team's, and the manager's objectives. Although it can sometimes be the conversation no one wants to have and everyone tries to avoid, it's not the one to rush or shorten in any way. I had to learn this the hard way. If objectives aren't easily understood and agreed to, you will be in for a lot of follow-up meetings to clear things up and gain commitments that you failed to get at the onset. Take the time upfront to ensure full commitments to goals, activities, and behaviours. There is no shortcut on this one.

This is easier with commissioned salespeople than with other staff. With commissioned people, you can simply ask, "How much do you want to make this year?" Salespeople can connect with objectives by breaking them down to weeks and months and translating them into income based on weekly and monthly unit sales. Once you get them to agree on the unit sales required, you can focus on the activities and behaviours necessary to achieve the targets. You can even focus on what activities and behaviours are required to get one unit sale and then determine the total required for the month. Relating goals to their income personalizes it for them and makes the commitment part easier. If for whatever reason their goals are not where you want them to be, you can give them a raise and increase their activity. In my case, seldom have I heard salespeople say they didn't want to make that much money. A great manager never dictates the goals but creates an environment where salespeople choose their own. It's your job to influence them to choose goals that are challenging for them and will ultimately meet corporate goals.

When it comes to managing those in non-sales roles, it's still a matter of getting employees to make commitments. The same principles found throughout this book will still apply in a remote-management environment. The key difference is in how you communicate.

I've been a manager since I was twenty years old, when I worked for a little finance company in Ajax, Ontario. I was too young for the bonding agency to insure me but old enough for the company to put me in charge of the entire operation and hold me accountable for everything, including the administration staff, which was the only other employee who happened to be old enough to do the banking. Over the years, I always seemed to be the manager of something; more often than not, I was managing people, a responsibility I have always enjoyed.

Dictionary.com defines a manager as "a person who has control or direction of an institution, business, etc.," or "a person who controls and manipulates resources and expenditures." It defines a leader as "a guiding or directing head, as of an army, movement, or political group." Neither one speaks to the responsibility of helping people achieve success. My personal definition is that leaders point in the direction we are headed, and that managers get you there.

Chapter 21
The Bully Manager

By Mario Carr
President, Carr Marketing Group

This is my personal story of dealing with a horribly inept and destructive boss. This boss was a bully in all the familiar ways, and this story reflects the bully's impact on me as an employee. I'm sure many of you can relate, and I hope you as a manager will learn from the experience from an employee's perspective.

Bullies exist everywhere. Recently, the bullying phenomenon in schools has been receiving significant press, and rightly so. Do these bullies grow up and retain their propensity to be bullies when they join the workforce? Are we expecting more bullies to move into management and negatively influence employee performance?

Over the last decade, there has been an increase in bullies in the workplace. According to the Canadian Health Council, one in six people are now being bullied at work. It all begins with the hiring process. We hire people who seem to be high performers because managers want quick fixes. Like the rest of society, managers want instant gratification, so they hire those who seem to get things done in a hurry with great success. Bullies are often assertive in an interview, coming across as confident in their skills and appearing quite competent. It becomes an easy decision to unwittingly hire a bully.

But then something goes terribly wrong. The new manager's staff want to change departments or quit the company altogether. Turnover increases in their departments, and employee surveys indicate serious problems. Quality of service and production usually suffer, but the bully is an excellent manager when managing up. Supervisors become convinced that the bully is doing a great job but needs better people. The bully also blames the issues on others. The truth is that the high performer that everyone thought was a superstar is the one causing havoc within the organization. The great hire turns out to be the bully from hell.

Some bullies aren't found out for years because they know how to hide in the organization. People who work for the bullies are often discouraged from telling anyone in fear of losing their jobs, and HR usually drag their heels in dealing with them because bullies are so convincing in defending themselves and shifting blame.

My Story

A number of years ago, a friend of mine arranged an interview for me, and I landed a job. He worked at the company and became my boss. After a few months, this so-called friend of mine turned on me. He turned out to be a nasty bully towards me, which went on for two years.

He would send nasty emails to me that sounded like he wanted to fight. Every time I responded to these, he would send out another one that was even nastier. He would constantly tell me what a bad job I was doing and that if I didn't smarten up I would be in trouble. He would even yell and scream at me about doing a lousy job and that I was lucky to even have a job.

I was deathly afraid of losing this job, so I worked hard to improve on what I thought was wrong. It made no difference, however, as he was always angry with me and verbally abused me. He still sent out the nasty emails and would still scream at me in front of other employees. I thought he was trying to help as a friend, so I would try to improve. I didn't make the connection yet and was influenced by my thinking he was my friend. I thought he had my best intentions at heart, and I excused his behaviour because of the pressures of his job. I was actually enabling him, and the attack emails continued.

I never told anyone at work about this because I didn't want people to know that I wasn't doing a good job. This went on for two years until one day I approached the bully's partner and told him the situation. He told me that I was doing a good job as far as he was concerned, and he had no problem with me. I even told him that I wanted to quit. I told him that I would prefer flipping burgers at McDonald's than putting up with the bully. He promised to help by talking to my boss.

Apparently the conversation worked, as the nasty emails stopped for about two months. After that time, however, I received another attack email from my boss. They started to flow again on a regular basis and so did his yelling at me in the office. I couldn't take it anymore. I was losing sleep and worried for my job, so I went to my doctor to discuss the situation and asked for his advice. My doctor suggested a night school course at a local community college on how to deal with difficult people.

I thought about taking the course before asking myself why I should spend my time and money on a solution for a problem that isn't mine. It's the bully's problem, I thought, and that's when I had an epiphany. I realized that my so-called friend was thriving on attention. I came to the conclusion that the worst thing I could do to him was nothing at all. That's right: nothing at all. If I didn't respond and just ignored his emails and yelling, it would make him feel powerless.

This is the key point. Bullies want power, so take away their power. They thrive on attention and feel powerful by putting other people down. It seems their self-esteem feeds on their victim's.

As soon as I ignored my bully, guess what happened? The nasty emails and yelling stopped. I was right. In fact, he became extremely friendly. Despite that, I could hear a voice in my head saying how leopards never change their spots. I thought he was being friendly in an effort to win me over so he could bully me again. I was always courteous and professional but kept my distance.

I then talked about the situation with other employees in the company. I discovered I wasn't a unique case, as just about everyone had similar problems with him. I also learned that the company had lost some high-quality people to competitors because of him. In the end, the company lost. Ironically, so did he because he was a shareholder.

Once the bully realized I was onto him, he lost his power over me and couldn't threaten me anymore, so he focused his attention on other prey. He went after his partner and made his life miserable. In the end, the partner couldn't take it anymore and bought out the bully's shares and terminated his employment.

The buyout was costly. What's more, after the termination, the partner was threatened with a lawsuit and was under tremendous pressure.

Months went by, and the company seemed like one big happy family again. The partner was my new boss, and he was always friendly to me until one day his personality seemed to change overnight. He didn't seem to be approachable anymore, and he was always agitated. I think he was draining money out of the business in an effort to pay off his debt in buying out his partner. The balance sheet was suffering, and he needed to increase profits and lower expenses. This meant pushing his employees to the limit without any extra compensation. His response to his business crisis was to turn autocratic and make unreasonable demands from his people.

Now *he* became the bully.

His bullying tactics were different from his partner's. Instead of sending out harassing emails and yelling at employees, he would give you the impression that he was a nice approachable guy. He would seemingly empower you with the task of finding solutions to problems that ultimately pop up in any project. However, whenever I presented solutions, he would take weeks to decide and always discounted anyone else's ideas except his own. I had a certain area of expertise within the company, and he bypassed me completely to purchase new software that was supposed to make my job easier. Well, the new program didn't work, and when I informed him of the problem, he basically didn't want to be informed. He proceeded to tell me that it was now my problem and I had better figure it out. When I asked for help, I was ignored.

I had worked hard at the company for some time but was no software expert. The volume of work in my area had expanded four times in the past year, so a solution was important. However, because the boss made the decision alone and it turned out poorly, he abdicated complete responsibility and dumped the entire problem and the responsibility to fix it on me.

I went to the firm who installed the program for help, but they couldn't. They blamed it on a bug in our system. I was getting nowhere with a solution, and the boss refused to deal with me in a proactive way. All he did was attack me for the delays in processing and the declines in customer service levels. Other staff started to complain, and I realized that I was facing an impossible task and that I was on my own. My new bully took out his anger on me, and I realized I had no choice if I wanted to keep my sanity: I had to quit this job. He spoke with me about four days before I quit, and all he did was blame me for something that was really his fault. Bullies can be contagious. Even the other people I worked with became nasty. The actual work environment changed, and the culture became one of attack and blame rather than cooperation. This is one of the most severe problems that employing a bully can cause. It was a tough decision to leave this toxic environment with no job to go to, but I gave the boss two weeks' notice.

Even though I was with the company for some time and did a complicated job that required some training, they didn't hire anyone until three days before I left. I trained a woman they hired for the job, and she noticed almost immediately the unsavoury culture in the office. She sensed in a matter of hours that she would be forced to deal with bullies. She even asked me if there were any bullies in the office. I told her not too many.

We finished our first day of training, and she came back the next day. When she went for lunch, she phoned me and said, "I hate to do this to you, but I'm not coming back. I quit." She had just left an office with a bully culture and knew this company was going to be the same. She decided to keep looking for a good company.

On the day I left, the boss came over to my desk. Rather than wish me well in my career, he said, "You better get all that work on your desk done before you leave tonight."

In discussions with my former co-workers, the situation hasn't improved. It's sad that a company with great potential can be driven into the ground by bullying tactics and employees having to suffer this indignity to earn a paycheque.

The Future of Bullying

Bullying is increasing at our schools and at work. There is no easy solution to the bully problem in the school system, but as they enter the workforce, I think we will see less and less acceptance of this behaviour. New generations of employees are less driven by loyalty to a company and more driven by personal empowerment and work–life balance. Companies with a bully culture will continue to lose good employees and will lose their competitive edge. It's just poor business to have a bully in the workplace, and it's poor business to keep a bully in your company. I believe we will see their numbers and their impact reduced in time.

In the meantime, if you're a bully, stop and think about the consequences of your behaviour. If you're being bullied, stand up to the bully and leave the company. Show them this behaviour is unacceptable in the modern workplace.

As for me, I am now self-employed and don't have to deal with bullies anymore. It's empowering to be in charge of your own destiny, and it should be this way in all companies. Great managers empower and trust their people. They share the glory and recognize contributions. They ask; they don't tell. They build on employees' strengths; they don't destroy employees' based on their weaknesses.

The bully's days are numbered.

Chapter 22
The Personal Manager

By Draj Fozard

"You want me to do what?" These were the first words I said to Gary when he asked me to "guest" author and contribute to *Life Is Management*. As he proceeded to explain, I politely listened, but my mind was whirring like a hummingbird. I was certainly interested in and flattered by the opportunity, realizing perhaps a door was opening for me—a door that on my own I have not been able to open for various and very real reasons. But what to say? Oh, what to say?

You see, it was one thing to have been a purveyor of cubicle courage, with my motivational quotes ever so present. It was totally another to present myself as an example, to actually talk about me, myself, and I, to look into the mirror and ask the key questions. Well, folks, that takes confidence and personal courage. How would I tell the world what I really think? That I think the quip "It's not personal; it's business" couldn't be further from the truth when it comes to managing and leading real live people? (Actually, it's a load of crap.) There is not one business decision that doesn't affect people and not one "people decision" that doesn't affect people. Yes, we've all seen the slick vision/mission statements and exhaustive strategic and business plans, but without engaging the hearts and minds of those who make them a reality, they're just words— empty words if your manager has neither a heart nor a mind. Until we have real robots in the workplace, it's always personal. How could it be anything but?

Gary convinced me to write about the personal side of management (he can be pretty persuasive), and here we are. I figure my thirty plus years of leadership experience in various capacities have certainly taught me a few lessons along the way. In all honesty, most business and people issues boil down to three simple elements: engagement, alignment, and energy. I hope the following words of wisdom are just that. I hope these lessons will be of value.

Lesson One: Be Yourself

Being a personal manager means it begins and ends with you. You cannot change the essence of who you are. Sure, you can learn and get better at what you do and how you do it, but in the end, you are who you are. In other words, you can't change a cat into a dog, but you can strive to be the best damn cat in the neighbourhood.

I remember several years ago I hired a new assistant manager. She was certainly a bright light—positive, engaged, and knowledgeable. My instincts told me she had the right stuff to do really well; however, this was her first leadership position. I felt confident in my abilities to coach and mentor her, and as our relationship grew and strengthened, so did the open and honest dialogue. So it was no surprise to hear her say, "I'm really struggling here; I'm not very comfortable being the boss and telling people what to do."

I smiled to myself, remembering my first posting to the same position. I knew completely where she was coming from. We have in our minds the image of what a manager looks like (good or bad), and it's based mostly on our previous personal experiences with managers. There is much to be gained by working with different leaders. Everyone has their own style, natural talents, and set of strengths they bring to the job, but there is no such thing as a perfect manager.

I remember my own personal experience of being posted as an assistant branch manager at the tender age of twenty-four (fresh off of the trainee program). In less than a week, I issued warning letters to two employees—that was their first impression of me. Why did I do that? It's simple enough to figure out now. I thought I had to be tough and make sure everyone knew who was in charge. *Stupid* and *misguided* would be two words I'd use to describe my early leadership behaviours. So much so that when I was transferred, a parting gift was a new name tag engraved with "Dragon Lady." I'm not too proud of that, but the lesson served me well in my career.

My advice to rookie managers has and always will be: first be yourself. Play acting or thinking of yourself as a certain type won't last. It's unsustainable and insincere. Your people will see through you in no time. I was also told that who you are and what you have done to get where you are won't change as you progress in your career. Leverage your strengths and be true to yourself. Don't be afraid to let people know who you really are.

Bring your best self to the job every day, but above all else, be yourself.

Lesson Two: Be Polite

I know what you're thinking: What does being polite have to do with management?

The simple answer: everything.

In my years on the job, I have yet to find an example or an instance where being rude or callous rather than polite and civil would have yielded better results. I remember working with a manager in the early eighties, long before any "respect in the workplace" policies. He was rude, obstinate, and crass, a leader who used fear and intimidation to get things done. Quite simply, he was just a big bully. This was early in my career, and interestingly enough, one can learn just as much (if they survive) through this type of experience, and I did. I learned about how important it is to pay attention to the little things such as saying good morning to each of your employees. I observed how much more engaged people became when you treated them with respect and dignity regardless of the level of position. I'd be a rich woman today if I had a nickel for every time I heard this manager say, "They're just tellers."

Everyone plays an important role on a team, and being polite to each other (yes, including saying please and thank you) whether it's up, down, or sideways in the organization is not only appreciated, it's the right thing to do. I have the pleasure today of working with a colleague who, through her demonstrations of kindness and courtesy, has inspired me to pay attention and make an effort to take the time with people.

Being polite costs nothing, but the return on investment is priceless.

Lesson Three: Be Interested

Being a personal manager means taking a genuine interest in your people. This means being interested in them as individuals, not just employees. It's about learning about them, not just to increase their output on the job, but also to genuinely demonstrate that you care. That only happens when you take time to talk to each other. Yes, of course you should talk about the work, but also talk about their lives, their kids, their vacation, and their hopes and dreams! It doesn't matter what the topic is. What matters is taking the time to be interested.

Had I done this myself many, many years ago, I would have learned an important detail about a member of my team. You see, that small detail was a personal detail that I didn't think was important enough to fully understand. It was a detail that would have saved me years of twinges of regret.

A minor detail? I'm afraid not. One day, an employee's cat died, and she called to tell me that she wasn't coming in to work, as she was too upset. I gave her a hard time. Not ever having been a pet owner, I had no empathy whatsoever. I also didn't realize this was a lifelong companion, and they had grown up together—for over twenty years. She was heartbroken, and I couldn't understand why she was so upset and absent from work.

Would you believe that to this day—over twenty years later—I regret the conversation I had with her and that I didn't think before I uttered the words, "It's just a cat." Good Lord, who was I then? Had I taken the time to get to know her personally, perhaps I wouldn't have reacted the way I did. I still feel bad about it. If by chance you're reading this—you know who you are—M, I am so sorry and just want you to know it taught me a valuable lesson, one that has truly made me a better and more compassionate leader over the years.

Lesson Four: Be Open

We all face real change in our lives every day. Whether these changes or challenges are expected or unexpected, good or bad, a personal manager needs to be open. This is about the willingness to change how you view the world as you deal with change.

I believe being open includes being honest with myself and with others. I don't need to have all the answers, nor do I have to pretend I do. My feelings are my feelings, and I have every right to stay true to them and make decisions that are right for me. This, of course, comes with its share of risk. These risks may change the course of your day, or your career!

In 1989, I was appointed to my first branch manager position. I was thirty-three years old and felt all my hard work and dedication was finally paying off. The branch needed serious attention on many fronts: people and processes and premises. Over the next two years, I devoted myself to making it a great place to work and to bank! We achieved that and more. We did so well that one day my manager called me to congratulate me on our stellar results, and he proceeded to advise me that a promotion was in store! It was a promotion that involved me commuting to a larger branch further away. It was thirty minutes further, making my drive over an hour each way. Not good.

Remember my story about the cat? Well, had my manager taken the time to get to know me, he would have discovered what was important to me personally—what I valued and what my hopes and dreams were. You see, by that time, I was thirty-five years old, and I was a single parent raising two young sons aged three and five living in Grimsby without any immediate family nearby. Had he known me better, he would have realized that time was my currency and taking care of my boys and being there for them was what I valued most. He would have known that my career aspirations included moving closer to home, not further away. He should have known that I would turn down the promotion. Instead, he was shocked that I did and told me quite frankly, "You won't get another chance...not for a long time." I was open and honest and told him how disappointed I was that he knew so little about me. Did I take some risk there? Absolutely. But I had to be true to myself and to the organization.

So how did it end? Well, my manager was partially right. They left me there for a couple more years. The risk paid off though, and my next move actually brought me twenty minutes away from home.

Lesson Five: Be an Example

Be an example. It's easy to say, but it's also easy to do. Maybe the point I want to make here is be the right example. But how? It really is a simple formula requiring only two ingredients: you and your actions. This means taking accountability for your own behaviour at work and realizing that you're being watched. Like it or not, your every move, your tone, and your demeanour are always centre stage.

I have found that managers often fail to understand how powerful they are and how their actions and general disposition affect their team. If a manager walks in and is in a miserable mood and lets it show, it will set the tone for the rest of the day if it's not otherwise salvaged. In such a case, needless energy will be spent on trying to decode the problem. The employees' focus will be misdirected, and productivity will ultimately suffer. I have witnessed this many times in my career.

I have also observed how powerful the right behaviours and actions can be. It's incredible how effective something so simple as being positive, personable, and consistent can be in engaging the hearts and minds of employees. The personal manager knows that creating a great working environment is all about the people. Regardless of the type of business or the products and services being sold, when all is said and done, we are in the "people business."

When employees see you working just as hard as they are, they will work harder. When your employees see you calling customers by name, so will they. My advice to rookies has always been to not expect your people to do anything you're not willing to do yourself. Employees knowing what is expected of them and there being no "say/do" gap is a powerful combination. Personal managers always walk the talk.

Being a great example on a team can make all the difference in the world. Over the years, I have had the pleasure of working with some amazing individuals on some amazing teams. The best teams all had individuals who brought their best self to work every day. It was through these experiences and projects that I fully realized and came to appreciate and understand the power of a high-performing team. They are the teams that bring out the best in everyone and know how to truly leverage individual talents. More important, they collectively and collaboratively get the job done—on time and on budget. It was through them that I learned to be open to new ideas and new ways of problem solving.

Lesson Six: Be Confident

Why confidence? Of all the qualities of a manager, why would I pick this one to focus on? I admit I did think long and hard and asked myself how it would fit into the theme of the personal side of management, and then it came to me. If you're confident, if you're in control of how you react to things, then your employees will gain confidence when they look at you—they will be in control too. Confidence comes from within. Confidence is personal. It's leading by example and a whole lot more.

I've reported to many managers over the years—some confident, others not so much. The managers who were confident in who they were as leaders ("be yourself"), the ones who were able to make decisions under pressure, and the ones who were willing to take an unpopular stand on an issue were the ones I remember and the ones who made a difference in my career. They challenged me and put me out of my comfort zone, but because I was confident in them and their guidance, I learned and thrived.

A confident manager is just what you want during turbulent times and periods of great change. No one wants to follow a manager unable to instill confidence and calm, no matter how nice or open they are. Confidence is too important. Future leaders will be facing new and different challenges, but the goal of leading and managing through change remains the same: get through it safely. You need confidence in yourself and in your people to do that.

An important lesson in building confidence that I learned was when I reported to Gary. There I was, just weeks into a new position and assigned the task of creating a new loss report. (Isn't it amazing how one remembers something that happened almost sixteen years ago?) I worked hard on it and thought it was complete. As I presented it to him, even before he read it, he asked me point blank, "Is this the best you can do?" At the time, I didn't realize the power of that question. I remember being hesitant in my response to him and starting to qualify my answer. He then proceeded (with a flourish, of course) to tear up my report—all my work! I was aghast. How dare he! And with that grin and oh-so-direct gaze, he said to me, "I want your best." I've carried that lesson with me and coached others on it. Perception is reality. Be confident!

Lesson Seven: Be Present

Simply be present. I chose this lesson for two reasons. First, it reinforces the previous six lessons. It would be useless to practice the other lessons without truly being in the moment—simply showing up. Second, being present means active listening, paying attention, and focus. These are all activities that make the art of management much more personal. It's hard work requiring genuine effort and deliberate intent. The challenge is to remain in the present and not get distracted with the regrets of yesterday or the worries of tomorrow. Being present means embracing the here and now and mindfully leading and managing in real time to bring out the very best talents of your people.

One More....

Finally, through it all, I have learned the most valuable lesson of all: I learned to accept the fact that change is my constant companion and will always be waiting at the doorstep. It's always better to embrace and invite change than to fight it. Acceptance is a marvellous thing that ultimately allows you to move forward. It's not important whether you agree with the change, only that you accept it and get on with your life. One of my VPs many years ago told us we really only had two choices: agree or accept.

And speaking about lives, my life has had its fair share of challenges, both professional and personal. I have come to believe that everything happens for a reason, to take you to something better or to save you from something worse. I've smiled through better, and I've survived worse. I have the smile lines and the scars of a full and exciting life to prove it. I know I have made positive contributions to the people and world around me. For me, being successful simply means finding new doors to open, doors to push wide open with courage and confidence!

This is the story that has shaped my leadership and managerial style today. Sure, it has worked for me, but more important, I have influenced the careers and lives of many co-workers over the years. That is the best reward and endorsement I could ask for.

So there you have it. This is pretty simple stuff, yet it's amazingly powerful when put into practice. I'm an avid practitioner of practicality, of sharing concepts and ideas people can really use. It was a delight for me to have had this opportunity to look back on my working career, to think about what wisdom I could impart and share with you. I also know that all of this is just as applicable on a personal level at home as it is in business. Trust me.

Thank you, Gary, for giving me this opportunity. I appreciate it more than words can say.

Sources

Aronson, Elliot, et al. *Social Psychology*. 7th ed. London: Pearson, 2009.

Bennis, Warren, and Joan Goldsmith. *Learning to Lead: A Workbook on Becoming a Leader*. New York: Basic, 2010.

Bickman, Leonard. "The social power of a uniform." In *Journal of Applied Social Psychology*, 4(1), 1974: 47-61.

Buckingham, Marcus, and Curt Coffman. *First, Break All the Rules: What the World's Greatest Managers Do Differently*. New York: Simon & Schuster, 1999.

Carnegie, Dale. *How to Win Friends and Influence People*. New York: Simon & Schuster, 2009.

Cialdini, Robert B. *Influence: The Psychology of Persuasion*. New York: HarperBusiness, 2006.

Cialdini, Robert. *The Power of Persuasion*. VHS. Stanford: Stanford Alumni Association, 2001.

Collins, Jim. *Good to Great: Why Some Companies Make the Leap… and Others Don't*. New York: HarperCollins, 2001.

Covey, Stephen, R. *Seven Habits of Highly Effective People*. New York: Free Press, 2004.

Drachman, David, et al. "The extra credit effect in interpersonal attraction." In *Journal of Experimental Social Psychology*, 14, 1978: 458-467.

Festinger, Leon, et al. *Social Pressures in Informal Groups: A Study of Human Factors in Housing*. Stanford: Stanford UP, 1983.

Ford, Gary L., and Connie Bird. *Life Is Sales*. Toronto: Insomniac, 2008.

Friedman, J. L., and S. C. Fraser. "Compliance without pressure: the foot-in-the-door technique." In *Journal of Personality and Social Psychology*, 4, 1966: 195-202.

Gladwell, Malcolm. *Outliers: The Story of Success*. New York: Hachette, 2008.

Heath, Chip, and Dan Heath. *Switch: How to Change Things When Change Is Hard*. Toronto: Random House Canada, 2010.

Kulka, R. A., and J. R. Kessler. "Is justice really blind? The effect of litigant physical attractiveness on judicial judgment." In *Journal of Applied Social Psychology*, 4, 1978: 336-381.

Mack, D., and P. Rainey. "Female applicants' grooming and personnel selection." In *Journal of Social Behavior and Personality*, 5, 1990: 399-407.

Mercer, David. *IBM: How the World's Most Successful Corporation Is Managed*. London: Kogan Page, 1987.

Merton, Robert K. *Social Theory and Social Structure*. New York: Free Press, 1968.

Miller, Alan S., Satoshi Kanazawa. "Ten Politically Incorrect Truths About Human Nature." In *Psychology Today*, http://www.psychologytoday.com/articles/200706/ten-politically-incorrect-truths-about-human-nature,accessed February 25, 2013.

Mintzberg, Henry. *Managing*. San Francisco: Berrett-Koehler, 2009.

Moriarty, T. "Crime, commitment, and the responsive bystander: Two field experiments." In *Journal of Personality and Social Psychology*, Vol. 31(2), Feb. 1975, 370-376.

Regan, Dennis T. "Effects of a favor and liking on compliance." In *Journal of Experimental Psychology*, 7, 1971: 627-639.

Rosenthal, Robert, and Lenore Jacobson. *Pygmalion in the Classroom: Teacher Expectation and Pupils' Intellectual Development*. Bancyfelin, Carmarthen: Crown, 2004.

Sheikh, Fawzia. "Sales Meetings That Don't Suck." In PROFITguide.com, http://www.profitguide.com/manage-grow/sales-marketing/sales-meetings-that-dont-suck-30311, accessed February 25, 2013.

Sinek, Simon. *Start with Why: How Great Leaders Inspire Everyone to Take Action.* New York: Portfolio: 2011.

Zenger, John H., et al. *How to Be Exceptional: Drive Leadership Success by Magnifying Your Strengths.* New York: McGraw-Hill, 2012.

Contributors

Connie Bird
(Chapter 18: Coaching to Achieve Business Results)
Connie is an executive coach currently working with specialized sales. In the last three years, she has coached leaders on strategy execution and behavioural coaching that lead to business results. Her experience in the financial industry includes retail banking, commercial banking, and financial planning. She is currently coaching sales force leaders.

Connie is the co-author of *Life Is Sales*.

Gary Laughlin
(Chapter 20: Remote Management: Managing What You Can't See)
Gary is the president of GHL & Associates. His company specializes in sales coaching for mortgage professionals to increase their referral business through centres of influence, in particular realtor referrals.

Before his current role, Gary was vice president, mobile mortgage specialists at RBC. He was instrumental in launching, building, and managing this national sales group for RBC.

Gary has spent his entire career managing people and in particular developing people to reach their potential.

Mario Carr

(Chapter 21: The Bully Manager)

Mario has more than twenty years of experience in public relations and communications. Some of his email marketing campaigns have received responses within minutes. He heads the Carr Marketing Group and is the director of public education for the Hamilton Amateur Astronomers. He writes a blog and a monthly newspaper column on astronomy and appears on CHCH-TV to talk about the night sky. He is also on the Communications Committee for the Burlington Chamber of Commerce and is a Rotarian.

The Carr Marketing Group brings sales and marketing together to help businesses grow. These are the two keys to success for every business. As a public relations, email marketing, and communications firm in Burlington, we help companies develop a profile and translate it into sales. We also provide crisis management, marketing strategies, environmental communications, investor relations, event planning, speeches, etc.

For more information, please visit www.carrmarketinggroup.com.

Draj Fozard

(Chapter 22: The Personal Manager)

Born in former Yugoslavia, Draj moved to Canada as a young child and grew up in Northern Ontario. She holds a degree in economics from McMaster University and obtained her Certified Financial Planner designation in 1998. A vibrant and successful leader with over twenty years of senior leadership experience, she has never stopped fulfilling her desire to learn and to inspire those who work with her to achieve their potential. From taking MBA courses part-time to taking piano lessons to participating in community theatre, she is always engaged in rewarding experiences and is now pursuing her Human Resources Certificate at Mohawk

College.

Outside of the academic realm, Draj is invigorated by her love for travelling, music, and her two adoring sons, Michael and Nicholas. She currently lives in Grimsby, Ontario, with Sam and Lily—her two cats!